GOAL SMASHER!

LIFE AND CAREER

MAGGIE WORTH

Goal SMASHER! Life and Career

Print edition published by Wheat Germ LLC 2018
Newnan, GA

Paperback Edition
ISBN 978-1-945095-17-7

Introduction
Important – and short!

Goals. Virtually everyone has them and most of us spend a good chunk of our lives and careers trying to reach them. Let's be honest: that last part can be pretty frustrating. When goals fail, most people blame themselves for not trying hard enough, or attribute failures to situations outside their control. And sure, in some cases, either or both may be true. But, I've been working in strategy for a very long time, and I've found that the majority of goal failures are actually the result of faulty planning, not lazy execution. It's kind of the old "garbage in/garbage out" concept. If you don't set the right goals – or create an execution plan that you can actually carry out – how can you possibly hope to get a good outcome?

That's where Goal SMASHER! comes in. It's the product of almost five years of research, development, testing, and revision, and it really truly works! It's comprehensive enough to get the job done right, but straightforward enough to actually follow. The philosophy is simple: if you plan better, you can do more. Whether you're working toward a promotion, a new career, financial security, early retirement, educational or lifelong learning aims, an empty-nest strategy, or virtually any other dream you want to make reality, this system will work for you... *if* you follow the process and put in the necessary time and effort up front.

Goal SMASHER! is *simple*, but it isn't necessarily *easy*. It requires intense thought, often of the kind we're unused to or uncomfortable with, and a willingness to look inward with a good deal of honesty and curiosity. It also takes time. You are unlikely to sit down with this book and work out a strong plan in a few days. You'll need to give yourself time to think, to reflect, and to walk away occasionally so you can come back with fresh eyes and a rested mind. So, if you're looking for something quick, or something that doesn't require much effort on your part, this system probably will not work for you. If you truly embrace this process, you *will* work hard, but it will also be worthwhile.

That said, most of the work is done up front. You'll work hard to develop the plan, but the system is designed so that you aren't constantly trying to adjust it or remember what it means, or figure out what you're supposed to be doing. Once you've got the plan, working with it day-to-day is neither difficult nor time-consuming (though, of course, some of the tasks you set for yourself might be). Also, remember that the first few times through the process require the most energy because you'll be learning to think very differently. Like any tool or skill, the more you use this system, the more natural it will become and the faster and easier the process will go. You'll still be putting in the same *amount* of thought and work, but the work itself will be easier and less time-consuming for you to accomplish.

Ultimately, the decision to try Goal SMASHER! comes down to this: are you genuinely passionate about reaching your goals and committed to creating the strongest possible plan for getting there? If so, read on. If not, that's okay! But you might want to put this book back on the shelf until you're ready for it. The system will not work if you don't.

About Goal SMASHER!

Read if:
- *You're trying to decide whether this book is right for you*
- *You're curious about why I developed Goal SMASHER! and how it's different*
- *You just like reading all the sections*

Before we start working the system, let's take a minute to address some common questions for those of you who want answers. (If that's not you, go ahead and skip to the system summary, located just before Section One.)

Why do I need a goal plan? Can't I just make a list of goals and work on them?

You can. Many people do. Sometimes it even works. More often than not, however, this stripped-down approach generates more frustration than fruit, particularly if you're trying to achieve something difficult, complicated, or significant. Lists are ideal for lots of things: shopping trips, packing for vacation, getting through a day with lots of things to do, remembering all the books you want to read or movies you want to watch, paying the bills, etc.

I genuinely love lists. I make them all the time. And, in fact, the Goal SMASHER! process starts by making a list. The key is that it doesn't end there. If you really want to reach your goals – and reduce the chance of doing so only to find it wasn't what you really wanted after all – you need a strategy of attack. That's exactly what you'll have when you finish the work in this book.

Aren't there plenty of goal-setting systems out there already? Why another one?

Sure, there absolutely are other systems – and one (or more) of them may work for you. That said, my experience has been that the majority of popular goal-setting approaches don't work very well in the real world.

The core problem is that popular approaches rarely cover all the bases. To begin with, most systems assume that goal-setting in life is fundamentally different than goal-setting in business. This is completely false.

True, the nuts and bolts are different, and so is the context. Executives setting company goals will necessarily write down different things than an empty-nester who wants to write mystery novels. The two will have different sets of pressures, different sets of people to whom they're accountable, and different constraints and resources. They may also require the use of different language and terminology. Goal-setting in a major organization absolutely looks and feels very different than goal-setting for an entrepreneur, for a high school student, for an individual focused on advancing their career, or for a person setting life goals.

That's why I've published different versions of this book: to more effectively speak to groups with similar interests and challenges. Each version uses language and examples specific to each audience, but the Goal SMASHER! system, itself, is the same in each one. That's because, while the *environment*, the "stuff," surrounding goals can be quite different in these various scenarios, the *underlying process* for creating a workable, effective strategic goal plan is virtually identical.

We've trained our brains to think business life and personal life are two totally separate worlds, however. As a result, goal-setters (and a lot of experts) typically use vastly different systems, all of which tend to be incomplete. Methods and mindsets surrounding life and personal goals are often very abstract, very focused on living and feeling, which can leave people with a whole lot of motivation, but not much in the way of action items. Corporate goal-setting techniques almost always err in the other direction; they're big on actionable, measurable plans, but tend to ignore the living, feeling human beings tasked with carrying those plans out. The first type focuses too much on the big picture and the second focuses too much on the nitty gritty. Both are out of balance, and both are likely to cause much stress and frustration for the user. More importantly, neither is likely to result in long-term success.

Further, most systems, including those that do incorporate both the abstract and the concrete, are either far too simplistic way too complex. On top of that, most approaches are either strictly linear (which is horribly limiting) or very free-form, which is a nightmare for linear thinkers (who represent the vast majority of the population). Frequently, they're either too flexible to be useful or too inflexible for real-world living.

I've also found that the steps in many models aren't placed in the best order in terms of the user thinking through the process. Finally, most systems help you write your plan and then wish you the best of luck. You're on your own when it comes to implementation. This book includes an entire section on working with your plan once it's complete.

I understand these many mistakes well, because I committed all of them at some point while trying to come up with a workable system for my clients. And that, right there, is the essence of why I wrote these books: Goal SMASHER! works.

What's so special about Goal SMASHER!?

Goal SMASHER! is different because it:

- Is designed for real-world use by human beings, even in less-than-ideal circumstances
- Results in a plan you can fit into your daily schedule with minimal stress
- Considers both the big picture and the details – and ties the two together

- Helps you set the right goals, for the right reasons, before you start working toward them
- Creates specific, practical actions you can incorporate into daily, weekly, and monthly to-do lists
- Accepts that the best-laid plans can be interrupted or disrupted by things outside our control – and helps you anticipate and plan for them when possible
- Addresses the need for outside help, support, and/or resources
- Uses positive reinforcement to increase engagement and motivation
- Provides insight on how to use the plan once you have it, including daily use, assessing your progress, and making changes when needed
- Is comprehensive, but not complicated; you have to do a lot of thinking, but the steps aren't difficult to understand and the process is laid out so you'll end up with a streamlined, easy-to-follow document
- Works for almost anyone, whether you're a Fortune 500 CEO setting corporate goals, an entrepreneur trying to get your business off the ground, or a private individual who just wants a better way of defining and reaching your life dreams

- Is a great professional development tool for existing and emerging company leaders, but can also help kids as young as elementary school learn to think critically and strategically (with some assistance)
- Is extremely scalable, so, once you get the steps down, you can use it for something as extensive as a five-year plan or as simple as a telephone call
- Has been researched and tested; real humans have used it and found that it works

And who are you again? Why should I trust you?

First, please always ask people this question before taking their advice. And if they don't want to answer, run. Run fast, in the opposite direction. In my case, I have three main qualifications: experience, education, and inclination.

Both my undergraduate and graduate work was highly interdisciplinary, so I spent a lot of time exploring how psychology related to English, sociology related to physics, and so on. That background exposed me to a lot of different ideas, systems, and philosophies – and all of them came into play as I developed Goal SMASHER! I've also completed extensive training in life, career, and executive coaching, hold an International Coaching Federation credential, and am MBTI® (Myers-Briggs) certified. Additionally, I've read and analyzed literally hundreds of articles, books, studies, and blogs about personal, entrepreneurial, and corporate goal attainment. Add in dozens of seminars, trainings, and workshops on negotiation, selling, communications, and more, and my total body of related learning is fairly significant.

In terms of experience, I spent almost 22 years in a variety of corporate, small business, and higher education roles, most of which required a huge amount of strategic thinking, planning, and execution. During that time, I built the third-largest merchant-owned ATM program in the country, broke and grew two new sales territories (one global), created one marketing department and completely restructured another, managed projects ranging in size from a few thousand dollars to more than $20 million, trained and mentored more than 150 total employees and interns, and developed policies and procedures for everything from university crisis communications to homeowners' associations. I also drafted countless business, communications, marketing, and implementation plans, and wrote more than a dozen training manuals, text for hundreds of ads and marketing documents, and almost a thousand features, how-tos, and information pieces for newspapers, magazines, and online outlets. I wrote one textbook for hire, complete with test prep, and served as technical editor on another.

For the last five years (including a three-year overlap with my last higher ed administration role), I've workshopped and provided consultation on strategic planning with a number of small businesses and entrepreneurs, and also privately coached individuals, creatives, and small groups. I've spoken and taught face-to-face and online, through university continuing ed departments and private associations, on topics including strategic communication, goal-setting, professional and business writing, creative writing, and more. I've even published fiction, which taught me a whole other set of skills and gave me a completely new set of tools and systems to draw from. The point is that I've done a lot of different things – and all of it has helped inform how I approach, coach, and teach goal-setting.

More important than education or experience, however, is the fact that I'm naturally inclined toward the kind of thinking that makes for good goal-setting. Everyone has their gifts and that's mine. Don't ask me for a physical description of a person I just ate lunch with, or for directions to a restaurant I've visited a hundred times, or how to calculate compound interest. You *will* get an incorrect answer. My social skills are iffy, my EQ is unreliable, and I'm a disaster at interpersonal relationships. I'd be a terrible ambassador and a worse grief counselor. But I'm a really, really good strategist, and goal-setting is just a form of strategic planning. I sort of came pre-wired with the ability to see interesting connections between seemingly unrelated things – and to figure out how to create new and useful things from those connections. Realizing this, my grandfather, who was both an artist and an engineer, taught me about perception, interplay, and synergy while I was still in preschool. He helped me write my first personal strategic plan when I headed into middle school (although he didn't call it that). His mindset and mentality stayed with me in everything I did from then on out. In short, I was born to be a strategist and wise people nurtured my natural ability. At this point, strategy is as much who I am as what I do. (If you're an MBTI® aficionado, I have a very strong preference for INTJ – which basically means I'm really good at coming up with systems and am driven to make them work in the real world.) Since I've also been gifted with the ability to explain big, complex things in an approachable way, I have a unique opportunity to help other people develop their own strategic planning skills so they can get more of what they want out of life – with less stress.

That's what Goal SMASHER! is all about.

System Summary

Goal SMASHER! is a nine-step, acronym-based process, broken down into six sections:

Defining goals (Goal, Significance, Measures)

Adding details (Actions & Schedule)

Addressing potential problems (Hurdles)

Covering needs (Energy & Resources)

Rewards (!)

Each step includes an important core question:

Goal - What do I want?

Significance - Why do I want these things?

Measures - What does success look like to me?

Actions - What steps can/will I take to reach my goals?

Schedule - When will I take these steps?

Hurdles - What might get in my way and how can I deal with it?

Energy - How will I sustain morale and motivation?

Resources - What do I need in order to reach these goals?

! (Rewards) - What can I look forward to having/getting at the end?

The process begins with some critical pre-work. Do *not* skip that part.

At the end, you'll find an additional section devoted to working the plan and assessing it. Don't skip this either.

Again (I can't overstate this), don't skip or combine steps! You need them all to make this work and it's not as intimidating or difficult as it might sound at first.

At the very end of this book, I've placed a sample 30-day timeline for working through it. Note that this is an aggressive timeline, and you may need to adapt it (possibly significantly). If the idea of planning already makes you tense, don't even look at the chart; it's just a suggestion anyway. It's totally okay to do this thing at your own pace.

One more important note: all the examples contained in this book are just that, examples. I'm a strategy specialist, not an attorney, financial advisor, healthcare provider, etc. You'll need to select specific goals, actions, etc. based on your personal needs/circumstances, and in consultation, when necessary, with qualified professionals who can help you determine what's wise, healthy, and financially sound for you.

Let's get started.

Section One: Prework
Don't skip this! Seriously.

Earlier, I said that writing bad goals results in bad outcomes. It's also true that going into goal-setting badly prepared results in bad goals. You need to start with the right tools and the right mindset. That's what this section is about, and it's incredibly important that you do this work before you start the Goal SMASHER! process.

Individual clients working toward personal or career goals often come to me with what they think is a problem achieving goals. What I typically hear is, "I'm great at setting goals, but I can never seem to reach them. What's wrong with me?" In virtually every case, the answer is the same: nothing is wrong with you, but you're not great at setting goals. You're great at writing down a bunch of stuff you want to do and then tackling it. That's not strategic and it's not likely to get you where you want to go.

About half of my individual clients initially resist the idea of writing a full goal plan. I often hear "I don't want a whole plan. I just want to make a list of goals and work on it." I get that. But it's not working for you or you wouldn't be here. As you may have read in "About Goal

SMASHER!" I love lists, but making a list is only the very first step in goal-setting. If you stop there, you'll be frustrated forever. It comes down to this: you will expend at least the same amount of time and effort making endless ineffective lists as you will doing it right in the first place. So either invest the time and effort to plan correctly up front or waste the time and effort trying to use a method that very rarely works. That's a decision you have to make before you begin. You absolutely have to be ready to try something different or this system will not work for you.

Further, particularly in corporate environments, I see a lot of people who view goal-setting as a necessary evil, something that has to be done so they can check it off their lists and move on. They just want to put something on paper to show they met the requirement, and then they typically ignore the whole plan until they have to report results. Oddly, I see a number of small business owners and entrepreneurs with this mentality, too. Somewhere, an advisor or business book has told them that they should set goals, so they go through the motions, but aren't really invested in thinking it through or working the plan once it's finished. This kind of just-get-it-done mindset almost always launches a vicious cycle wherein the crummy goal-setting yields crummy results, so the setter becomes convinced goal-setting is a waste of time and is even less invested the next time around. If you're still approaching goal-setting as something to check off your list, this system will not work for you.

As I said before, if you truly embrace this process, you will work hard, but it will also be worthwhile. Anyone can learn to set good goals, but you have to be ready. That's why this section is critical.

Physical Stuff

The good news is, you don't need much in the way of supplies. However, working through Goal SMASHER! will require you to write at every step. I realize this is the digital age and I'm a huge fan of sustainability, but I encourage you, in the strongest possible terms, to go old-school with this and write longhand with an actual pen or pencil and paper as you work. Hand-writing actually does engage a different part of the brain than typing. And, as virtually every professional writer on the planet (and a whole lot of trainers, teachers, coaches, and psychologists) will tell you, the physical act of writing connects you to the words more intensely. It also allows you to jot and cross out and amend without erasing your earlier thoughts, which can be helpful to review from time to time. In addition, the resulting list will be more personally meaningful because it's in your own handwriting rather than in impersonal, generic computer font. Plus, of course, you're less likely to get distracted by social media and email notifications if you aren't sitting on your computer or device.

Any notebook or paper (or really big whiteboard) that suits your fancy will work. If you want to periodically type up and save your notes to ensure they don't get lost or so that you can easily share them with others, absolutely do so. Also, a lot of people like to create an electronic version of their final plan once it's set. But unless you have a condition that makes computing or dictating necessary, I really want you to try writing longhand while you work through the process, even if you think I'm being silly.

Speaking of dictation, your mind also processes information it hears differently than information it reads – even when you're the one saying the words. Get in the habit of reading your notes aloud, either to yourself or to someone else. You'll be surprised at the way it affects your understanding of what you've written.

Mental Stuff

The main tool you'll be using for this process is your brain, so it's critically important that you get in the right mindset before you start. There are three core skills you'll need to employ to make Goal SMASHER! work for you:

Patience. It really is a virtue, especially when you're trying to be strategic. As I said in the optional introduction, you're not going to finish this process in a day or two. If you do, I can guarantee that you've short-changed yourself.

Occasionally, I run into someone who needs to read through the entire book first to get the big picture. This only works for a very small number of people, however, and you probably already know if you're one of them. Most people find it much more helpful to start at the beginning and work step by step without reading ahead. Regardless of which type of reader you are, when you actually begin working through the process, you need to give yourself adequate time to work on every single step. Don't rush, work the steps in order, and do not skip or "combine" steps. Every step is important, every step is there for a reason, and every step deserves your wholehearted attention. That said, I do recommend you set yourself a reasonable time limit for completing your plan, especially if you really enjoy planning and have noticed you have a tendency to plan forever and never do. It's important to plan properly and with patience, but if you don't move on to execution, there isn't much point. Four to eight weeks works for most individuals (corporate teams are a bit different).

Consistency. Life loves to throw curveballs, and you can't possibly anticipate or avoid every interruption, but do try to start this process when you know you'll be able to focus on it regularly over the course of several days or weeks. Picking up in the middle after a week or two can be tough, and a lot of people never get started again once they pause. For some folks, even a couple days away from the project is enough to derail their efforts. If you know this is you, commit now to spending at least 10 minutes on goal-setting every single day until you've finished your plan. You don't have to be writing or reading during those minutes – in fact, most of the time, you won't be. As I mentioned before, effective goal-setting requires a lot of thought and you need to dedicate uninterrupted time to simply thinking if you want to see success.

Honesty. At several points in this process, you'll need to ask yourself some tough questions. If you're not honest about the answers, which includes being realistic about your time, abilities, and potential stumbling blocks, you'll set yourself up for failure. It might be easier and feel better in the short-term, but it won't pay off in the long run. Remember that we're talking about your life or your career here. Aren't those things worth honest consideration?

Optional Stuff

If you've got something to write with and on, and you've engaged your mindset, you've got what you really need. I do, however, want to make two more suggestions because they've worked so well for my clients.

Picture it. I'm a big fan of visualization, not only to help achieve the goals you've set, but in the initial goal-setting process, itself. From time to time, take a moment to try to picture in your mind whatever you're writing or saying aloud. If your goals list includes earning a promotion, picture what that might look like. If your reasons list includes seeing your grandchildren graduate college, imagine that as well. Yeah, I know, this is going to sound hippie-dippy for a lot of folks, especially if you aren't naturally inclined toward this sort of thing. I get it. I used to think visualization was bunk, too. Then I discovered that it works, and why throw out a tool that works? It might seem uncomfortable at first, but I promise you it's not the tool, itself, but rather your unfamiliarity with the tool. Try it a while and you'll probably become a convert like I did (which will probably annoy you no end for a while, as it did me). Just stick with it, it's worth it, I promise.

Buddy up, it works! You may find it helpful to find a feedback partner, a friend or colleague who is also working the Goal SMASHER! process, or even to form a small (no more than four to eight people) feedback group. We often learn more by explaining an idea to someone else than we do by reading about it ourselves. You can also gain surprising insights from listening to others work through their own processes. This is why I workshop the system in small groups whenever possible.

One last note: If you have a life coach, mentor, or therapist, I'd encourage you to share your work with that person as well. This is particularly true if you are in therapy to manage an ongoing condition or because you're in a difficult place right now. The goal-setting process, as I've developed it, is deeply introspective. Taking it on when you have an unmanaged condition, or during a time of crisis, is not necessarily a good idea. Please talk to your therapist before beginning so you can decide together whether this is the right time – and the best method – for you.

That's your prework. Now, let's get going on your goals.

Section Two: Defining Your Goals
Three steps.

One of my biggest frustrations with traditional goal-setting is that it spends so little time ensuring we've identified the right list of goals before rushing off to decide how to reach them. It assumes that we know exactly what we want, what it looks like, what it means, why it's important, and whether it's even a good idea. That's a whole lot of assumptions. And they frequently turn out to be wrong.

Have you ever started working on a goal and thought, "Hang on. What I really should be working on is..."? Have you ever reached a goal only to realize you didn't really want it or that it didn't accomplish what you thought it would? Do you find yourself constantly tweaking your goals because you can't remember quite what you meant when you wrote it down, or because you realize it's unrealistic, or it's way too narrow, etc.? Have you ever looked at a goal and been unable to decide whether you reached it or not? These things happen all the time. All. The. Time. And it's not because you can't do this. It's simply a product of not taking steps to identify and define your actual goals before diving in.

So that's where we're going to start, because if you don't have a clear idea of your destination, you can't possibly set a good course for getting there. This section includes three steps. Essentially, you're going to decide what you want to do, why you want to do it, and what success looks like. When you get to the end, you should have a solid list of three to five goals. Then – and only then – we'll start thinking about how you can reach them.

Step One: Goal
This is the "Goal" in Goal SMASHER!
Core question: What do I want?

Work: Create a list of possible goals
Why: Because where else would you start?
Mindset: Think big-picture. This is about vision.
End Product: List of 10-20 possible goals to choose from (don't freak out, step two will reduce this to a more manageable number)

If you're still reading this book, you're interested in setting goals, so I'm not going to spend time talking about the importance of having them. I do, however, want to take a few minutes to define what a goal is and isn't, because it's not as straightforward as it seems.

In broad terms, a goal is anything you want to do or accomplish. Effective strategic goal-setting starts broad, then narrows, so we're going to start out thinking about the big picture. Goals should be aspirational and inspirational, not detailed or specific. I realize this approach runs directly counter to one of the most popular and widely-revered goal models out there, the SMART system. So let's take a short detour and talk about why.

If you've done even a tiny amount of work or research on goal-setting, you've heard of SMART goals. The idea behind the SMART concept is that goals should be specific, measurable, attainable/achievable, realistic (or relevant, depending on the source), and timely or time-bound. While SMART is certainly not the only highly concrete system out there, it's by far the most popular and I have to say I'm not a fan. I'm not alone in my skepticism, incidentally. Business experts and life coaches seem pretty well divided about the effectiveness of SMART goals, and many therapists, psychologists, and other mental health professionals have suggested that the SMART system has the potential to do more harm than good.

In short, SMART is too surface-level and too binding to be used for strategic goal-setting. It doesn't consider the big picture, and doesn't ask why. It doesn't work well for goals that can't be measured in numbers. As a result, while SMART seems straightforward and simple, it can actually get complicated and confusing quickly. In my experience, people who rely on the SMART method for strategic goal-setting have a tendency to get hung up in the mechanics of the system and fixated on meeting all the qualifications, which results in setting goals that don't really reflect what they want to achieve.

That's why I'm not a fan of SMART *goals*. SMART *actions*, on the other hand, are a pretty good idea. When we get to steps four and five, you'll note that Goal SMASHER! uses a lot of the same principles as SMART.

Actions should be concrete and specific. *Goals* should be big and they should stretch us.

Work Time
Task: Brainstorm Big Goals

Task: List 15-25 goals you want to achieve
Do: Think big
Don't: Prioritize
Don't: Go into detail or try to be overly specific

Pull out your handy notebook and start brainstorming. For now, I want you to simply make a list of what you want to achieve. Don't worry about whether it's measurable. Don't worry about the size or scope. Don't worry whether it's "right" or what other people might think. It's perfectly okay to jot down both "replace my laptop" and "improve my craft," even though the first one might not sound like a goal worth planning toward and the second may feel too broad. It'll work out, trust me. It's also okay to include both overcoming impostor syndrome and landing a film deal if that's what you want to do. You might aspire to be able to write full time, sign with a particular agent, attain a certain income level from writing, learn to balance family, personal, and writing time, go more marketing, etc. Or you might write down that you want to write books you love. Whatever it is you want, just let it flow. And yes, you can absolutely have both life and career goals on the same list and in the same plan. Work is part of life and vice versa — and that includes work associated with your writing.

If you end up with a list of ten things, keep going. About twenty is ideal. If you hit 30, rein it in for now. You can always add more later. When you finish, your page should look like this:

1. Goal
2. Goal
3. Goal
4. Goal
5. Goal
6. Goal
7. Goal
8. Goal
9. Goal
10. Goal

...and so on, up to 30. Once you have your list, turn to the next page of text in this book. Remember that you can walk away and come back later. In fact, it works best if you do exactly that. Give yourself a day or two to mull this over. Perhaps ask a partner or close friend what interests and goals they've heard you express. They may remember things you've mentally pushed to the side but want to revisit. If you have trouble getting started, try these prompts:

- In my ideal life (or career), I would...
- When I look at my career (or life), what's missing is...
- I've always wanted to...
- In the next five years, I'd really like to...
- I'd feel successful if I...

Now, head off to work on those lists!

Wishes

Got your list? Terrific! Before we leave this step, we're going to refine that list a bit to remove or repair two common problems. The first is wishes.

I've found that people often have a difficult time distinguishing between goals and wishes, which are also broad and aspirational. Goals are things you can actively pursue; wishes are things that happen to you or in spite of you. Wishes are awesome. We all need them. But, while we can sometimes increase the chances of their coming true, we can't really work toward them or achieve them without some luck. It's important to take wishes out of your goals list, or to change them into something you can achieve. Otherwise, you may do all the work and invest all your energy in reaching a wish, but never get that critical piece of luck. That way lies frustration and disillusionment. So let's go ahead and sort them out now. Feel free to start yourself a "wish list" somewhere else if you like. I have one and I engage with it regularly. Just don't confuse it with your goals.

So, how do we tell wishes and goals apart? Remember that a goal is anything you want to do or accomplish. This choice of active verbs is intentional. Goals should focus on things you have the power to make happen. You might have to work very hard, stretch a lot, and ask other people for help. You might have to sacrifice and take many actions building up to your goal. But it has to be something you can actively work toward and achieve.

For example, winning the lottery is not a goal. Yes, you can do things to make it more likely that you will win (even if only marginally so). Specifically, you can buy tickets. And that's about it. You can run statistical analyses until your fingers fall off, but the outcome is ultimately based on chance. This means it isn't a goal. Winning a game show or contest that's based on knowledge or skill, on the other hand, could be a goal because you can study or practice.

A client once pointed out that game shows aren't entirely in a person's control, even when based on skill rather than chance. What about all the game show scandals in which the outcome was rigged? While the argument may seem like splitting hairs, my client brought up a valid point: in the end, very little is one hundred percent within our control. If we focused solely on the things we could control absolutely, we'd never get anything done. There's always death and accident and disaster and, yes, crooked game show producers to consider. We kind of have to let those things go, both in goal-setting and in life.

The game show example prompts another interesting question, however. What if someone else studied harder or developed greater skill? Hmm. Okay, to some degree that's in our control, but to some degree it isn't. So is it a goal or isn't it? We can work toward it, but we can't be certain of attaining it, even if flash floods and dishonesty don't intrude. This brings us to a truth that's often incredibly difficult for people to swallow at first: it is okay to not meet your goals.

Now that you've picked the book up off the floor and have, I sincerely hope, stopped cursing my name, let's talk about this. I say it's okay to not meet your goals for a number of reasons:

Goals are a target, not a destination. It's okay to land somewhere in the general vicinity. This is another of my problems with SMART and similar systems. Over-emphasis on reaching specific, quantifiable measures sets people up for frustration and a sense of failure. Under SMART, if your goal was to win the show and you only came in second, you failed. Period. Game over. When you look at goals as targets, though, you can realize that second place is pretty spectacular and be happy with what you've accomplished.

Goals are meant to stretch us. If we only set goals we could surely achieve, we'd never get further than "walk to the refrigerator" and "type my name." Neither is much to shoot for. The most fulfilling goals carry an element of risk in that you may fall short, and an element of challenge in that you have to really work to get them.

Goals can change. This is particularly true of long-term, big-picture goals. Something like seventy percent of college students change their majors at least once. These days, it's the norm for adults to have at least one major career change in their lives. All this happens because people grow and change throughout their lives. Their goals should evolve with them. But goal changes can happen even in the short-term and that's okay.

Goals aren't imperatives. Sometimes they seem to be, particularly when it comes to work and business. But, overall, you really shouldn't be working toward something you don't want. When we get to steps four and five, we'll start seeing more imperatives. Sometimes you have to do stuff you don't want to do in order to get what you want. Most of us do have to make a certain amount of money in order to pay our bills. Most of us have to plan around family and other commitments. But setting a goal you don't actually want to achieve is a great way to make yourself miserable.

So, if it's okay to not meet our goals, what's the point of setting them in the first place? Why put in all the work to think strategically and explore our inner reasons if we don't care about reaching the goal in the end? First, understand that I didn't say you shouldn't achieve your goals. In fact, there's a good chance you'll meet many of them bang-on. I'm simply saying that it isn't an all or nothing proposition and that it's okay to change your mind along the way.

Second, your best shot at getting what you want still comes from strategic goal-setting. We all need something to aim for or we just sort of wander around accepting whatever comes our way. That's no way to live a life or develop a career.

Finally, it's important to realize that the real value is in the *pursuit* of goals, not in their *attainment*. I know this sounds cliché; "life is a journey, not a destination" and whatnot. But remember that many clichés become clichés by being true over and over again. This is one of them.

Also, understand that I'm not talking about an "A for effort" or "participation trophy" mentality here. My point is that, as I mentioned earlier, when we get too hung up on meeting a precise goal, we miss out on the fun, the learning, and the value of the actual work we put in toward the goal. The long list of scientific and technological discoveries made while attempting to do something else proves this beautifully.

And don't forget that achieving a goal is a momentary victory. You'll spend far more of your life working toward it than actually realizing it. If you don't enjoy the work, it's going to be a tough haul. If you're going to hate every moment of memorizing endless sports and literature trivia in order to win a gameshow, you might want to pick a different goal.

So, games of skill: goals. Games of chance: not goals. You need to set goals you can work toward, not goals based on luck. If it's completely (or almost completely) outside your control, it's a wish or maybe a fantasy. Wishes are fine. Wishes are great. They just aren't goals. Let's practice.

Which of the following is a goal based on this principle? "Living to be 100" or "living in a way that extends my life." If you said the latter, you're right. Granted, living to be 100 sounds grander and sexier (and look, it's also specific and measurable!), but achieving it relies on far too many variables outside your control.

That said, there's something inherently motivating about setting grand goals, particularly if you're going to be sharing them with others or using them as inspiration – and especially if you've made peace with the "goals are a target, not a destination" concept. So once you have your final goals list in place at the end of step three, feel free to add more motivating nicknames to your goals, like this:

Goal: Live in a way that extends my life (live to be 100)

Or even:

Goal: Live to be 100! (live in a way that extends my life)

You can do this with career goals, too, if you like:

Be the boss! (earn a promotion to manager)

Or

Be the boss! (start my own business)

This kind of motivating language genuinely works for some clients. If that's you, do it – after step three. As we work through these first three steps, however, I want you to be very intentional in the way you phrase your goals. For now, write down the actual, in-your-control goal, in this case "living in a way that extends my life." Doing so will keep you – and your feedback partner/group if you have one – from getting confused along the way.

Work Time
Task: Weed Out Wishes

Task: Evaluate each item on your list and remove or revise any wishes
Do: Think critically
Don't: Overthink; you can come up with a reason anything's impossible if you try hard enough

Pull out your goals list and read it through, looking out for anything that's a wish, rather than a goal. Unless you wrote something completely uncontrollable such as "win the lottery" or "become immortal," however, I don't want you to cross the wishes out. Instead, think about ways you can reframe them into goals. Continue reading when you're finished.

Not-Goals

We need to check our lists for one more potential hazard: the infamous not-goal. This isn't a real term; I made it up. However, it perfectly describes a tendency some clients have to set negative rather than positive goals. Examples I've really heard:

- Don't lose my job
- Don't fail biology
- Don't lose the client/bid
- Don't turn into my mother/father

Perhaps you can see the issue with these. If not, let me explain. First, they all focus on the negative. Every time you look at them, you can't help but think of the terrible things that could happen. Talk about a morale-killer. Second, these goals don't aspire to achieve something, only to avoid something. You may turn 40 without turning into your parent, but then the question becomes: who are you? "Not-parent" is not a person.

You have a choice to make in the case of not-goals. You can, if you so choose, simply reframe them:

- Keep my job
- Pass biology
- Keep the client/win the bid
- Be different than my mother/father

These are all okay goals (maybe not the last one). But they could be better. The issue is that you're still focused on the negative outcome, you've just reworded it to sound more positive. And in some cases, there may be issues beyond your control, which means you have goals that are actually cleverly disguised wishes. If the client's budget gets cut, you may be unable to control whether you keep the business. If the coursework is simply too challenging for you, you may be unable to pass, no matter how hard you work at it. In these cases, you need to set a related goal that you can achieve. You cannot guarantee that you will pass the class, but you can set a goal of doing your absolute best. You can't guarantee that you won't lose the client, but you can make yourself or your product so valuable that you're tough to let go.

I also want to talk about the top and bottom goals in this list from a deeper perspective. While I can live with these goals, I don't love them, because they place emphasis on someone other than you. Keeping your job makes your company more important than you are. I would rather you set a goal of finding a job from which you aren't constantly worried you'll be let go. This puts the emphasis on your health and happiness, while still keeping your income intact. I'd rather you focus on becoming your own person, whoever that may be, than on being different from some other standard. Always put the emphasis on you and on what you want to achieve.

Work Time
Task: No More Not-Goals

Task: Evaluate each item on your list and remove or revise any negative goals
Do: Think critically and deeply
Don't: Hold back because it's hard

Pull out your goals list again, this time looking for not-goals. Reframe or delete, just as you did with wishes. When you finish, you should have a list of 10-20 goals that you can actually work toward and that reflect what you want in your life and/or career.

Tip: leave several blank lines – or the equivalent space – between goals; it'll make the next step easier.

Once you have your list, turn to step two, and we'll begin talking about significance.

Step Two: S
Significance
Core question: Why do I want these things?

Work: Identify the meaning behind each goal, and narrow your list
Why: To ensure you've got the right goals in place
Mindset: Honesty. This is about understanding your motivation and identifying patterns.
End Product: Refined list of 5-10 goals (we'll cut strategically once more in the next step)

Ever heard the question "what's your why?" The idea behind it is to identify your core motivation or your core reason for doing something, to answer the question "why is this significant?" – why does it matter. That's what we're doing in this step, and it's important for two main reasons.

1. To understand why you want each goal
2. To see if you have larger, underlying goals you haven't spelled out

The first is important for several reasons. We're going to refer back to significance later, first when we look at energy and again when we talk about reward. In this step, however, understanding the significance of a goal helps you clarify the goal, itself – and helps ensure you're setting the right goal based on what you need and want. Both contribute to your ability to succeed – and reduce the chance that you'll waste time and energy on goals that don't get you where you want to go.

The second is important because of the tendency I mentioned earlier of people to get too specific during the initial phases of goal-setting. I often work with clients who are frustrated because they simply have too many goals. The full list is overwhelming and they have no idea where to start. Most of the time, however, when we start digging into each goal's significance, we find that they really only have three or four big goals; all the other things are just actions or secondary goals that contribute to the big goals. (We'll talk about secondary goals in the next step.) Once they put everything in perspective and understand what really matters to them, most people are able to create goal lists that are far more approachable. That, in turn, means forward movement and that leads to success.

In this step, we're going to take five total passes at the list you wrote in Step One: Goals. Bear with me and actually do them one at a time. There are valid reasons we do each separately, and in order. Follow the process and you'll have a much clearer picture of your goals at the end of this step.

Work Time
Task: What's Your Why

Task: Identify why each goal is significant (pass one)

Do: Think seriously about why each item matters to you

Don't: Be afraid to discover your goals aren't quite what you thought they were

This first part is pretty straightforward, though the mental and emotional work can be tough. Below each item on your list, simply write down why it's important or what it does for you. It might look like this:

Goal: Earn a promotion
Significance: It pays more

OR

Goal: Earn a promotion
Significance: I'm tired of paying rent

Note that you may have more than one why associated with some or all of your goals, like this:

Goal: Earn a promotion

Significance: It pays more

I'll have more responsibility

I can learn new things that will help me continue to grow

OR

Goal: Buy a house
Significance: I'm tired of paying rent

I'm tired of having people living above me

I want to be able to paint my walls

I want a yard for my kids (or future kids, or dogs)

Okay. Go to work. You can use "significance" or just "S," or even "why," if you prefer, to identify them. When you've finished, turn to the next page and we'll begin refining.

Have-Tos

Ask any coach, therapist, or savvy manager about the best ways to kill motivation and morale, and you'll hear the same thing over and over again: take away choice. In fact, one of the most frequently repeated laments I hear from clients is "I don't have a choice" or "I have to do this, but..." In actuality, we almost always have a choice, even when it doesn't feel like it. If you really look at all the things about which you feel you have no choice, you'll find there's almost always an "if" attached.

Examples:

"I have no choice but to stay in this job I hate... if I want to pay my mortgage."

"I have to work 14-hour days... if I want to keep this job."

"I have to quit smoking/start exercising/eat healthier... if I want to live longer."

"I have to go to college... if I want to become a doctor."

I'm not saying all these aren't viable reasons to do something. But they are, in fact, reasons, and they do reflect choices. You're choosing the hated job over possibly losing your house. Is that a rotten choice to have to make? Sure. But it's a choice nonetheless. And, as soon as you acknowledge that you have a choice, facing the lesser of two evils becomes automatically a little easier. It gets even easier still when you remember what we said about Not-Goals in Step One and realize that what you want is to keep your house – and that you want to keep your house because it's an investment, because it provides security for your family, etc. Again, this is one of those things that may initially feel like splitting hairs, but it does make a difference.

All that is to say that "because I have to" is not a valid why, at least not by itself. Again, I'm not saying you don't actually need to do something, be it for personal or financial reasons. But the real significance lies in those reasons, not in the fact that you're being compelled to do it. For example, you might need to complete a course of education or earn a credential in order to be considered for a promotion. If you've listed earning that credential or completing the course as a goal, you may be tempted to write "because I have to" or "because it's required" as the significance. Please don't. You'll be much better served – and have much more chance of success – if you look more deeply at your motivation. In this case, your list might look like this:

Goal: Earn my certificate in ____
Significance: I'll be eligible for promotion

                  I'll learn the skills I need to be confident in my new job

It will add credentials to my resume in case the promotion doesn't come through

Now, compare that to:

Goal: Earn my certificate in ____
Significance: My boss says I have to

See the difference? The first version has numerous benefits over the second one:

- It gives a clearer picture of why you want what you want
- It acknowledges your choice and gives you options
- It's far more motivating
- It's focused on you, not your boss

This applies to personal goals, too. Let's go back to buying a house. If that's one of your goals, and you can't qualify right now, it might be tempting to write something that looks like this:

Goal: Get out of debt
Significance: I have to so I can qualify

Isn't it better to say:

Goal: Get out of debt
Significance: It will help me buy a house

It will improve my credit

It will give me more disposable income to do things

I want/help build savings

I will be less worried about paying the bills every month

Work Time
Task: Ditching No-Choice Whys

Task: Review your list for have-tos and replace with choice-focused options (pass two)
Do: Be willing to acknowledge that sometimes we choose between two not-great options, but there's a reason one is more acceptable to us than the other. Find that reason.
Don't: Skip this. It will make a difference.

Once you've finished this task, turn to the next page and we'll refine again.

Stopping Shoulds

After "have to," "should" is probably the word I hear most often from clients struggling with goal attainment. This can also be phrased as "supposed to." The number-one problem with "shoulds" is that they come from someone other than you.

Take these common ones:

- I'm supposed to go to the same college my mom/dad/aunt went to.
- We're married, so now we're supposed to buy a house.
- I should want to be promoted and earn more money.

It's fairly easy to see where these goals originated: a family member, society, a boss, a spouse, etc. Somewhere other than the person who has to live with the goal and try to achieve it. That's a problem because it means you're pursuing someone else's goals, not your own.

Note that "should" and "supposed to" are simply warning words that mean you need to take a closer look. You may, if you think about it carefully, realize that you actually do want to go to that college, buy the house, earn the promotion, or achieve whatever else you're "shoulding" about. That's okay. It's not in your best interests to rebel against things you want simply because someone else has placed the expectation on you, any more than it's wise to do things you don't want to do for the same reason. Ultimately, you need to pursue the goals you want, regardless of anyone else's expectations. So if you discover that you've written down a "should," you simply need to reevaluate and figure out why that goal is significant to you independent of anyone else.

Note: "shoulds" can be sneaky. Take a look at the below sample conversation. I've had a version of this one with numerous clients.

Client: I'm so frustrated with myself. I'm supposed to be working on my Italian, and I'm watching T.V. instead.

Me: Supposed to according to whom?

C: My goals list.

M: Think back to when you wrote X on your list. Why did you choose that particular thing?

C: Because I want to be able to speak the language when I take my trip.

M: Okay. And why is that important to you?

C: Well, I read this blog and it said if I wanted to have an authentic experience, I should learn the language.

M: Other than that, is there a reason you want to learn Italian?

C: Well, no.

See what happened there? On the surface, this looks like a goal this individual set for themselves, but, when we dig deeper, we find it came from elsewhere. Again, this may or may not be a problem, depending on the situation. It's simply important to ask ourselves the question now so we don't waste time pursuing something we don't really want.

Here's why we do this now: at first glance, the above looks very much like an execution problem – and sometimes it is. The issue might also have to do with motivation or scheduling or energy or one of the other issues we're going to look at in later steps. But figuring out why you aren't reaching goals is very much a trouble-shooting process, and the first thing to look at is whether you set the right goal to begin with. Because, if you didn't, none of the rest matters. So, what we want to do now is make sure you haven't set a goal only because it's something you think you should do or should want. That way you won't waste time planning for that goal or energy trying to achieve it.

Work Time
Task: Stopping Shoulds

Task: Review your list for shoulds and eliminate or reframe (pass three)
Do: Be willing to challenge the status quo and/or ideas you've held for a long time
Don't: Fall into the trap of letting other people decide what you want

Take another look at your list and hunt out any "shoulds" that you honestly don't want – or don't want right now. Dump those, hard as it may be. If you've written a "should" significance, but you really do want to achieve that goal, you'll want to change your significance to reflect your own why rather than someone else's. Again, the actual process here is simple, but the mental work can be tough. Once you've finished this task, turn to the next page and we'll tackle the next refinement.

Clarifying Your Intent

Next we need to take an even closer look to make sure you've uncovered the core significance. In this pass at your list, you're going to look at each significance you've written and ask why again, this time about the significance rather than the goal, itself. The best way to explain this is to look at an example we used earlier. Remember this one:

Goal:	Earn a promotion
Significance:	It pays more
	I'll have more responsibility
	I can learn new things that will help me continue to grow

All three of these whys are great surface-level reasons to want to earn a promotion. But each individual why has a deeper significance. Why, for example, does it matter to you that the job pays more? This might seem obvious at first. Who wouldn't want more money in their paycheck? If we look more closely, however, we'll probably find a whole host of reasons why earning more is significant for you, personally. Maybe it's to achieve financial security. Maybe it's to purchase certain things or attain a certain lifestyle. Maybe it's because income level is a key part of your definition of success. Maybe it's all of these – or something else entirely.

Take a look at the second two whys in the above example. Can you see why respect may be important to different people for different reasons? How about learning and growth?

The key here is to figure out what matters to you. Again, this is important for two reasons. First, because we're going to use the results of this pass to narrow your goals list again in the next pass, and second, because we're going to use this information in two later steps. Note that there are no right or wrong answers as long as you're being honest. Your reasons may be very practical or a bit more aspirational. They might be a combination of the two. That's perfectly okay.

Also, note that not every goal and significance has to be terribly complex or lofty. Your whys may be quite straightforward for some goals, but more complicated for others. That's okay, too.

Work Time
Task: Clarifying your intent

Task: Review your list again ask yourself why each "why" matters (pass four)

Do: Write down all your thoughts, even if it's only a word or two. This will make the final refinement much easier – and your final goals list much stronger.

Don't: Hold back and don't delete anything. Just add to what you've already written.

Once you've finished this task, turn to the next page and we'll move on to the final refinement in this step.

Looking for Patterns

For many people, this is the most revealing task in this step. In fact, clients often report that this is the point at which they started getting excited about working through the rest of the system. What we're going to do is review your list again and start looking for patterns.

Patterns can show up in many forms. They might be repeated words, words that are similar to one another, or whys that are the same or similar between two or more goals on your list. They might also be ideas or themes that appear in multiple goals, or goals or whys that simply "feel" the same or similar to you. Tip: some people find it useful to highlight similar words/ideas in like colors.

Let's look at a career-based example. This hypothetical person has gone through each part of the process so far and is ready to start identifying patterns.

Goal 1:	Earn a professional certificate in ____
Significance:	I'll be eligible for promotion (*more money, more respect*)
	I'll learn the skills I need to advance (*increased confidence, makes me more valuable*)
	It will add credentials to my resume in case the promotion doesn't come through (*protect my income, give me options*)

Goal 2:   Get promoted

Significance: It pays more (*I can buy a condo, start saving more*)

I'll have more responsibility (*makes me more valuable, earns respect*)

I can learn new things that will help me continue to grow (*increases confidence and value, keeps me from getting bored*)

Goal 3   Grow my network of professional connections

Significance: So I can learn more about my industry (*keep track of trends, increase my value*)

To start building my reputation in the field (*increase respect and confidence, make me more valuable*)

To hear about new opportunities that might arise (*gives me options*)

Just in reading through this, certain repeated words probably popped out at you immediately. Words like:

- Money
- Confidence
- Value
- Options
- Respect
- Learning

You might also have noted some recurring themes based around these words:

- Financial security (money, ability to find a new position if needed)
- Job security (increased skills, knowledge, and value)
- Growth (in current role, personal finance, future job opportunities)

What this tells us is that this individual is focused on actions (get the certificate, earn the promotion, network) rather than bigger, deeper goals. As I've said before, this is a common misstep, one we've been trained to make over the course of our lives. It's the result of prioritizing "what are you going to do?" over "what do you want?" and it's a cart-before-the-horse mentality. Actions should be based on wants; the wants (goals) should always be in the driver's seat. Also note that "get promoted" may or may not be in this person's control. That puts the priority and the power with someone else, which we want to avoid whenever possible.

Let's look at how the person in our example might rework their goals. How about:

Goal 1:   Establish financial security

Significance: I'll have more control over my life

                I'll be less worried about losing my job

                I'll be able to buy things I want and save for my future

Goal 2:   Create job security

Significance: It will help me be financially secure

                It will help me feel good about my life

Goal 3   Grow professionally

Significance: I like learning and facing new challenges

                I want my career to keep moving forward

Can you see how this version of the list is more aspirational and big-picture? It also places the focus on and power with the goal-setter rather than someone else.

You'll note that most of what this person wrote in the first version seems to have disappeared. Spoiler: those things will come back, but as actions rather than goals. The point here isn't that the original list was wrong, just that it didn't go deep enough to identify what's truly important to the goal-setter.

To explain why this is important, I'm going to give you a glimpse into some of our future steps (stick with the process though; don't skip ahead!) At the very end, after we've worked the entire process, we're going to talk about using your goal plan on a daily basis. One of the things you'll be doing as you implement your plan is checking in to see whether you're on track. The way most people handle this is evaluation-based: did I check the things off my list? This is a yes/no, pass/fail mentality. The better choice is to use an assessment-based method, which looks like this:

Is this still my goal?

Yes
Are the actions I wrote helping me get there?

No
What should my new goal be?

Yes
Have I been taking the actions?

No
What actions should I be taking instead?

See the difference? When you assess, you're not simply looking to see if you did things, you're looking to see if your plan is still working and what you need to change to get on course. In order to do that, you need to have clearly defined big goals, supported by specific actions (Step Four). Big picture first, then the details.

Let's talk about one more important point and then we'll get to work on refining your goals. As we went through the example, you probably noticed that, to some extent, all of the goals and significances built on each other or connected in some way. That's one of the great secrets of the universe that surprisingly few people see: everything is connected to everything else in one way or another. My personal philosophy is that most of our problems and stress come from trying to separate life – and people – into nice, neat boxes that we can deal with one at a time. It doesn't really work and it causes us to miss out on a lot of connections and excitement. However, trying to deal with the entirety of the world at the same time can be utterly overwhelming – and also a reason people get frozen in inaction and don't get anything done. The key is to find a solid middle-ground, where you're aware of the big picture, but choosing to focus in on certain parts of it for a while. That's essentially what strategic goal-setting is about: understanding that the goals you set are interrelated and form part of the huge picture that is your life, but choosing specific areas to work on for a period of time.

All that is to say, don't get so bogged down in the connections between your goals that you can't choose your focus areas. This is easier said than done, and there's no hard rule for when to stop combining. As you get used to thinking this way, you'll develop a feel for it, though, so give yourself some time and space to do so. For now, aim to end up with five to ten goals. If you wind up with more, start looking for more commonalities. If you have only two or three, loosen up a bit and make sure you aren't setting goals that encompass too much territory.

Work Time: Looking for Patterns

Task: Look for patterns, then create a revised list with 5-10 goals
Do: Place priority on significance rather than the original goals you set.

Don't: Get so carried away that you end up with only one or two extremely broad goals

When you finish, you should have a clean list that looks like this:

1. Goal:
    Significance:

2. Goal:
    Significance:

3. Goal:
    Significance:

And so on.

Note that both your goal and significance may be new, and will likely be some combination or variation of the things you originally wrote. This is totally okay.

Two tips:

- Again, leave some room between each goal for the next step
- Do NOT throw out your old goals, significances, and other notes. We're going to refer back to them at least three more times before we finish this process.

Once you have your updated goal list completed, we'll move on to Step Three and finish our goal-identification work.

Step Three: M
Measures
Core question: What does success/reaching my goals look like to me?

Work: Define what success looks like for you and determine your final goals
Why: To further clarify goals and to provide ways for measuring progress and success
Mindset: Visionary and analytical
End Product: Refined list of 3-5 goals, with significance and measures identified for each

A quick note before we move into this section. By now, many people start feeling a little panicky because they've done quite a bit of work and still have no concrete action items. This goes back to the "get it done" mentality we've been trained to develop. It's completely normal (and okay) to feel a bit tense or at loose ends right now, but please resist the urge to skip this step so you can get to Actions. We will get there, very soon, I promise. I can also assure you that you will be better off pushing through your discomfort and following the system as designed. Everything will come together in the end!

If you're familiar with corporate goal-setting, you may be surprised to find this step near the beginning of the process. In more classic models, it's the very last step. However, defining success can be extremely enlightening and can be a valuable way to further refine goals and significance. Why wait until the end to put this tool to use?

I have two additional quarrels with the way measures are typically incorporated into goal-setting. The first goes back to the evaluation vs. assessment mindset we discussed in the Significance step. When you do all your planning first, then add measures, those measures are usually only useful in determining whether you executed the actions. If your actions stop working, you've set yourself up for failure. When you establish measures as part of the goal-identification stage, you can then choose actions specifically intended to get you to the goal as defined by your measures. This means that, once again, when you check in on your progress, you're asking whether the actions you identified are still moving you toward your goal rather than whether you failed or succeeded.

Let's look at this another way and picture your goal plan as a roadmap (and it is, FYI.) Say you decide you want to drive to Arizona to see the Grand Canyon (goal) because it's a national landmark (significance). Would you plan out which roads you're going to take and when you're going to leave without first plugging the Grand Canyon's address into your GPS or mapping program? Of course not. How can you decide how to get there if you don't know where you're going? Most likely, you wouldn't set off without at least knowing where you're going to stay when you get there and what hours the park is open. You might even decide whether you're going to take a tour when you get there, whether you want to take pictures, etc., because that might affect the time of year you choose to visit, what you need to pack, and more. Before you plan out the actions you need to take to get to the Grand Canyon, you're going to think about what you want your visit to look like.

Setting measures up front is the same thing. If you decide what success looks like, you have a much better chance of planning correctly than if you plan, then decide what success looks like.

My other issue with measures in the traditional goal-setting world has to do with quantitative and qualitative measures.

Quantitative measures are those that can be objectively evaluated:

- Earn an 80% on the test
- Make $50,000 a year
- Travel to nine new countries
- Reduce my workday by 10%

Qualitative measures are those that can't be objectively evaluated:

- Be happy
- Be more confident in my skills
- Feel less stressed about money
- Have more energy

If you've ever worked with goal-setting in a strategic environment, or used a highly concrete system, there's a good chance you've been told all your success measures should be quantitative. As a result, you've probably seen some really convoluted attempts to turn qualitative measures into quantitative ones. This is a horrible idea. It's a waste of time, it doesn't really work, and it's completely unnecessary if you simply accept that both qualitative and quantitative measures are valuable. In fact, the best goal-setting incorporates both kinds of measures.

The best way to illustrate this point is to talk about the one goal that consistently tops every list of common and popular personal goals in the U.S.: the seemingly universal weight-loss goal.

I have several friends who coach in the health, wellness, and weight-loss space, and they constantly struggle with clients who set only numbers-based measures. The chief offender is, "I want to lose X pounds." I get it (I've done it) and my colleagues get it too. Particularly when it comes to weight, we're absolutely conditioned to measure all success – and therefore all goals – by the scale. The first problem here is philosophical: why are we resting our happiness and healthiness on one number? That's the antithesis of big-picture thinking. That aside, however, the sad fact is that we are only limitedly in control of our body chemistry. We can't change our genetics. We can't change the structure of our skeletons. We can, however, put in the work to understand how our bodies function and to do the things we need to do to lose weight and/or become healthy.

So first, if you haven't already realized this, "lose weight" is not as effective a goal as "be healthy." I know very few health and wellness professionals who would not agree with that statement. Second, setting only quantitative measures for this goal (lose 20 pounds, lose 20 inches, reduce my cholesterol by 20 points) both creates a pass/fail mentality and also neglects the human component: what health feels like for you. At the same time, it's great to incorporate numbers-based measures because they're motivating and you can point to something concrete when you've reached them. The solution, of course, is to identify multiple measures, with some being qualitative and some being quantitative.

Let's go ahead and use the health goal to illustrate what this might look like:

Goal:	Be healthy
Significance:	I want to live longer
	I want to be able to do more things
	I want to like the way I look and feel
Measures:	Lose 20 pounds
	Reduce my cholesterol by 20 points
	Be able to run a 15-minute mile
	Have more energy

Be able to play with my kids/grandkids/dogs without getting winded

Feel more rested in the morning

Take fewer sick days/get fewer colds

Feel good in my clothes

See how this list combines both quantitative and qualitative measures? Some, of course, are somewhere in between. For example, you could easily quantify getting fewer colds. But you can't necessarily control that, and, honestly, will you really find "get three or fewer colds" motivating? Could you attempt to devise some sort of 1 to 10 scale that measures how good you feel in your clothes now versus how good you want to feel in the future? Sure. But why? It's completely unnecessary. You know when you feel better in your clothes. Trust that.

Another reason to use both types of measures is to manage morale and motivation. Let's say you set the above goal and put a six-month target date on it (we'll get to scheduling in Step Five). If you only set the quantitative measures, then get to the deadline and have lost only 19 pounds, reduced your cholesterol by only 19 points, and can only run a 16-minute mile, which are you likely to focus on: the progress you made or that darned one digit by which you "missed" every measure? What if, instead, you can see that you came within one number of meeting all three quantitative measures and also met every single qualitative measure on the list? How does that change your feeling of success? Your energy and excitement? Your motivation to pursue new health goals?

Some of you may be rolling your eyes right now because we've wandered into the realm of feelings. As a Keirsey rational, I understand your aversion. But the fact is, people are human and how we feel and are motivated contributes to success. Even if you look at it from a purely objective perspective, you'll see that motivated people who feel good accomplish more. And isn't that the whole point?

In this step, we're going to do two things. The first is to identify measures for each of your goals. Let's do that now.

Work Time: Identifying Measures

Task: Think about what success in each goal looks like to you and develop measures from that vision
Do: Choose both quantitative and qualitative measures
Don't: Forget to think about how success will feel as well

This can be a tough step for people to wrap their minds around. Remember, the core question is "what does success look like for me?"

When you finish, you should have a clean list that looks like this:

1.) Goal:
Significance:
Measures:

2.) Goal:
Significance:
Measures:

3.) Goal:
Significance:
Measures:

And so on.

Note that this is a great time to use visualization. Many people find creating a mind picture of success helps them identify the different components that contribute to the feeling. When you've identified your measures, come back to the text and we'll finalize your goals so we can begin the planning stage.

Finalizing Your Goals

You should have come into this step with five to ten goals. Ideally, you want a plan that contains three to five (maybe six). Any more than that becomes overwhelming. Do note that you may be working toward very specific things right now and therefore have only one or two goals. It that's the case, I'd encourage you to consider breaking them down just a bit so that you're in the three to five range. That way, you're not putting all your proverbial eggs in one or two baskets.

So, how do we get from five to ten to three to five? First, now that we have Measures to work with, we're going to repeat the Looking for Patterns exercise from the Significance step. Take a good look at the measures you identified and see whether any of the goals you've written separately should be combined. Once you've done that, it's time to prioritize. This really is exactly what it sounds like: deciding which goals you're going to work on now and which you'll save for the future. Other than the fact that you may have to reach certain goals before you can reach others, this is purely a matter of you thinking very honestly about what matters to you most and choosing the corresponding goals.

Before you do that, however, I'm going to give you a bit of an "out" in the form of secondary goals. You must, however, promise to use this tool sparingly and wisely. If you don't, you will overwhelm yourself and then be frustrated when you aren't able to take on everything at once. So, what are secondary goals? Essentially, secondary goals are smaller goals that build toward a larger one. The main purpose in a personal and career setting is to help you break big goals down into more manageable chunks if you need to. For highly detailed people, this is sometimes helpful.

Remember this example from the previous step?

Goal 1:   Establish financial security

Significance: I'll have more control over my life

                 I'll be less worried about losing my job

                 I'll be able to buy things I want and save for my future

Goal 2:   Create job security

Significance: It will help me be financially secure

                 It will help me feel good about my life

Goal 3   Grow professionally

Significance: I like learning and facing new challenges

I want my career to keep moving forward

What if this individual also has a goal associated with health, one focused on hobbies or travel, and another centered around family or relationships? Should that be six goals? Maybe.

Another alternative, however, would be to combine Goals 2 and 3 above, like this:

Goal 2:	Establish my career
2a	Create job security
Significance:	It will help me be financially secure
	It will help me feel good about my life
2b	Grow professionally
Significance:	I like learning and facing new challenges
	I want my career to keep moving forward

Note that, if you do use secondary goals, you can either attach Significance to the goal itself or to each of the secondary goals – whichever works for you. You can even do both if you like. You will, however, want to choose measures for each secondary goal. Let's look at our health example from above:

Goal: Be healthy
Significance: I want to live longer

I want to be able to do more things

So I can like the way I look/feel

Because you did the big brainstorming exercise in Step One, you've probably already identified several actions that you'll be choosing in the next step. For example, someone who set this health goal has probably already written down things like "exercise," "eat healthy," "cut out salt," "get enough rest," "manage my stress," etc. You could then, if you wanted to, set a health goal that looks like this:

Goal 1:	Be healthy
Significance:	I want to live longer
	I want to be able to do more things
	I want to like the way I look and feel
Goal 1a:	Improve my nutrition
Measures:	
Goal 1b:	Manage stress
Measures:	
Goal 1c:	Give my body the exercise and rest it needs
Measures:	

See how that works?

A couple of notes. First, don't set more than three secondary goals for any one goal. Second, don't set three secondary goals for each of five or six goals. You will end up taking on too much and becoming overwhelmed. Secondary goals are not intended to let you pack more than is reasonable into your list. They're mainly to help you organize yourself and your thought processes.

Work Time: Finalizing Your Goals
Task: Choose your final goals

Do: Check one more time for patterns, then prioritize

Don't: Freeze yourself in indecision because you are afraid you're choosing the "wrong" things. Remember, this is a plan. You can change it later if your priorities shift!

With the new information in hand, go ahead and choose your final goals for this planning period. Don't forget to check for patterns and combine as needed before you begin cutting. When you finish, you should have a clean list that looks like this:

1.) Goal:
   Significance:
   Measures:

2.) Goal:
   Significance:
   Measures:

3.) Goal:
   Significance:
   Measures:

And so on.

Or possibly:

    1.) Goal:
       Significance:
          Goal 1a:
          Measures:
          Goal 1b:
          Measures:

    2.) Goal:
       Significance:
       Measures:

    3.) Goal:
       Significance:
       Measures:

When you have your final list of goals, turn to the next section and we'll move into adding details with steps Four and Five.

Section Three: Adding Details
Two steps.

Good news! You've successfully made it through the toughest stage of goal-setting: identifying and clarifying your goals. From here on out, most of our work will be much more concrete. The two steps in this section, in particular, will be very familiar (and probably fairly comfortable) for most people. We're going to be choosing actions to help you reach your goals and setting a timeline for trying to achieve them. Another piece of good news: you'll probably find you've already identified a lot of actions when you completed your original goal-setting brainstorm. Huzzah!

More good news: you'll notice that this section contains far less explanatory text. Since these are pretty straightforward activities, we don't need to spend a lot of time talking about them before we start.

This is also the one section in which I'm going to tell you it's okay to go out of order – and to even combine steps if it works better for you. In fact, I'm going to recommend you read this entire section (this intro, plus Step Four:

Actions, and Step Five: Schedule), then decide which order you'd like to work in. Here's why:

Goal-setters generally fall into two groups:

1.) People who already have a specific timeframe in mind when they start, and
2.) People who have ideas about what they need to do but aren't sure how long it will take

If you're the first, you might want to set a tentative schedule, then go back and plug in actions by month, quarter, etc. Or, you might want to brainstorm a list of actions, then set a tentative schedule, then go back and plug in your identified actions based on that schedule.

If you're the second, you might simply want to focus on identifying the right actions first, then think about how long they'll reasonably take to accomplish and set your schedule accordingly.

In either case, you might back and forth a bit between these two steps before you complete both. When I workshop Goal SMASHER! in small groups, we do these steps together for that exact reason. It's completely okay. Do not, however, move on to Section Four (Step Six: Hurdles) until you've completed steps four and five. It's important that we complete this stage of planning before we tackle the next one or it won't work properly.

The most important thing to keep in mind while working these steps is to be realistic, both about what you can accomplish and how fast. If you take on too much, or try to do it too quickly, you dramatically decrease your chance of success. Don't do that to yourself from the beginning. It's okay to set some aggressive timeframes or some actions that will stretch you, but don't go overboard and don't make every action a stretch on a short timeline. Also, don't leave important, time-consuming actions out or you're likely to short yourself on time when you do your schedule. Note that, if you're using secondary goals, actions and schedule should attach to those rather than to the goal they're nested under.

So let's talk about the two steps in this section and look at some examples.

Step Four: A
Actions
Core question: What specific steps will I take to get me to my goals?

Work: Choose specific, doable actions that help move you toward your goals
Why: You have to do to get!
Mindset: Critical and concrete
End Product: Five to fifteen actions for each goal (or secondary goal)

Remember in the beginning when I said we'd talk about the SMART system later? Later has arrived. As I said before, my problem with SMART isn't the model itself, but the fact that it's used as an entire process rather than a way to think about one or two pieces of a more comprehensive process. When it comes to actions, SMART really is.

If you're unfamiliar with the acronym, it translates like this:

S - Specific
M - Measureable
A - Actionable
R - Relevant or Realistic, depending on who you ask
T - Timely or Time-bound

We're going to handle setting timelines in the next step, but we do want to think about the other aspects in this one.

When you choose actions, do make them specific. For example, this is not the time to say "develop healthy habits." Instead, you want to say "eat more nutritious food," "get adequate sleep," "exercise," "reduce my stress," etc.

Your actions should be things you can do (this is SMART's "actionable"). This means you don't want to choose actions someone else, like your boss or a partner, has to do for you (we've got a spot for those later, never fear!)

When it comes to R, I actually like both definitions commonly associated with SMART. You should be setting relevant actions, meaning you really need to think about whether the actions you choose will help lead you to your goal. And I've already pointed out the need to be realistic, a fact I honestly can't stress enough. With these things in mind, let's see what actions might look like. Remember our career example:

Goal 1:	Establish financial security
Significance:	I'll have more control over my life
	I'll be less worried about losing my job
	I'll be able to buy things I want and save for my future
Measures:	Be able to save 20% of my income each month
	Carry zero balances on my

credit cards

Feel less worry about money

Goal 2:	Establish my career
2a	Create job security
Significance:	It will help me be financially secure
	It will help me feel good about my life
Measures:	Excellent performance reviews
	Three months of my salary in savings
	Confidence that my boss considers me a valuable employee
	Grow professionally
2b	
Significance:	I like learning and facing new challenges
	I want my career to keep moving forward
Measures:	Confidence in my knowledge
	Promoted or moved into another role that pays 10% more

When we layer in Actions, they might look like this:

Goal 1:	Establish financial security
Significance:	I'll have more control over my life
	I'll be less worried about losing my job
	I'll be able to buy things I want and save for my future
Measures:	Be able to save 20% of my income each month
	Carry zero balances on my credit cards
	Feel less worry about money
Actions:	Pay off my debt
	Save money
	Reduce my monthly bills
	Increase my income, either by earning a promotion or finding side work
	Sell valuable things I don't use anymore
Goal 2:	Establish my career
2a	Create job security

Significance:	It will help me be financially secure
	It will help me feel good about my life
Measures:	Excellent performance reviews
	Three months of my salary in savings
	Confidence that my boss considers me a valuable employee
Actions:	Earn a certificate
	Attend networking events so I can develop new contacts in my industry
	Read articles and journals so I can keep up with industry changes
	Document my successes to help me earn promotions or secure new positions
	Take on tasks or projects that increase my value and visibility
	Grow professionally

2b

Significance: I like learning and facing new challenges

                     I want my career to keep moving forward

Measures: Confidence in my knowledge

                     Promoted or moved into another role that pays 10% more

Actions: Earn a certificate

                     Read articles and journals so I can keep up with industry changes

                     Take on tasks or projects that help me develop new skills

                     Ask questions and engage in conversations on industry forums or at events

                     Secure a mentor

Notice that three of the actions in 2a and 2b are the same or very similar. That's completely okay. The overlap shouldn't be total, but it's not unusual to find a few common denominators. In fact, it's great to find that one action can move you toward two (or more) goals. Do pay attention when this happens, though, because it means that action is very important. In future steps, you'll want to make sure you have what you need to take those actions. And when you're faced with prioritizing your to-dos on a day-to-day basis, remember which actions are most important. You can star those extra-important Actions in your plan if that helps you.

So now that we see what specific, actionable, relevant, and realistic actions look like, let's circle back and talk about what SMART calls "measureable." In the last step, I advocated for setting both quantitative and qualitative Measures for your goals. I still do. However, when it comes to Actions, I strongly recommend you still primarily, if not exclusively, focus on things that are quantifiable. This is rubber-meets-road time and you need a way to make sure you're moving forward. Think back to the Grand Canyon trip analogy. If you've plugged the Grand Canyon into your GPS, your GPS is going to tell you exactly how many miles to travel on each road, not "head down Route 5 for a while." Setting quantifiably measurable Actions is the same concept.

Let's look at the health goal we worked with earlier:

Goal 1:   Be healthy
Significance: I want to live longer
               I want to be able to do more
               things

I'll like the way I look and feel

Measures: 20 pounds down

Cholesterol down 20 points

Able to run a 15-minute mile
More energy

Able to play with my kids/grandkids/dogs without getting winded

More rested in the morning

Fewer sick days/ colds

Feeling good in my clothes

Actions: Eat 6 servings of fruits and vegetables per day

Reduce calories to X per day

Sleep at least 7 hours per day

Exercise for X minutes at least X days per week

Spend X minutes of the day reading/watching TV/playing with my dog/meditating

See how all of those Actions are quantitative? This allows you work very specific to-dos into your daily calendar down the line – and to adjust if you find you've over-reached.

Here's the other great benefit of quantifiable Actions: you can ramp up to them. Let's say your aim (which your doctor has approved) is to exercise 60 minutes a day, six days per week. You may not be physically capable of taking that on beginning day one. It's perfectly okay to set a series of measurable actions, something like this:

Exercise
    20 minutes, 5x/week
    30 minutes, 5x/week
    45 minutes, 5x/week
    45 minutes, 6x/week
    60 minutes, 6x/week

See how that works? As you may be able to anticipate, when we work with Schedule in the next step, you'll assign target timeframes for each measure. So (spoiler), it might ultimately look like this:

Exercise
    20 minutes, 5x/week - 2 weeks
    30 minutes, 5x/week - 2 weeks
    45 minutes, 5x/week - 4 weeks
    45 minutes, 6x/week - 4 weeks
    60 minutes, 6x/week - begin on X date

Remember that these are merely examples. Especially when it comes to health measures, you should always make sure any actions (and timeframes, and goals) you set are safe and appropriate for you.

One other note about measurable actions: it's perfectly okay to identify a range or an average. For example, our career goal-setter might write "attend an average of one networking event per month." Our person focused on health might write "eat 4-8 servings of fruits and vegetables per day."

So that's actions. Rather than pausing to work now, we're going to go straight into Schedule. After you've read that step through, you'll go to work.

Step Five: S
Schedule
Core question: What's my timeframe for completing my actions?

Work: Choose target dates for accomplishing actions
Why: To help you make regular progress rather than simply moseying along
Mindset: Realistic
End Product: Target completion dates assigned to each action

You've already gotten a sneak peek at what this step looks like. Functionally, it's just a matter of assigning a timeframe to each action and there isn't a whole lot more to say about this step. The biggest challenge will be deciding (realistically, remember) when you can start each item and when you want to finish by.

Do understand that, when we talk about "Schedule," we're talking about a broad schedule for, say, a year or two years, not about your actual day-to-day schedule. In the final section, we'll talk about some ways you can use your goal plan to set daily to-dos, but we're not there yet. For now, think in terms of Actions you want to work on in a certain month, quarter, season, year, etc. In fact, there are many ways you can handle this:

- Set a specific start and/or end date
- Set a date range

- Identify a week, month, quarter, or year

How you do that is completely up to you. Almost any measure associated with a definite timeframe will work. Use what's best for you, based on your life and what you want to accomplish. Just make sure that you stagger items a little so you aren't trying to do too much all at once, and keep in mind that some actions might have to be completed before you begin new ones.

A note about your end or completion date. Clients sometimes say "this is something I plan to do for the rest of my life or career, so there is no stop date." True. However, your goal plan really should have an end date. I typically recommend writing your plan annually, or every two years, because things change and you want to account for progress.

Granted, we're going to be assessing more often than that and potentially making adjustments, but if you don't start fresh periodically, you're going to end up with a crossed-out mess. Besides, it really is smart to completely rethink where you are and what you want from time to time. It keeps us in tune with ourselves and what's going on around us. So, if you've identified an action that you think will be ongoing for several years, simply give yourself a start date and set the end date as the date this current plan will end. You can always carry the action over to the next plan you write, but you may find you want to tweak it a bit at that time.

It's up to you to decide whether you're writing an annual plan, something shorter, or something longer. I write mine annually with my business plan corresponding to my fiscal year and my personal plan beginning and ending on my birthday. Because that works for me and I like the significance behind it. I do recommend you don't try to plan for more than three years at a time, however, particularly in a world that changes as frequently as ours does.

Work Time: Adding the Details
Task: Identify Actions with target dates for each goal
Do: Be realistic. (I'm really, really not kidding about this)
Don't: Get caught up in worry about whether you've identified the exact right Actions. Remember, we're going to assess these periodically and you can add/delete/change as necessary. Your goal plan is a living document!

So, I think we're ready to get started on steps four and five. Before you do, think for a minute about what order you want to do these in. Don't stress about it, however. As I said, a bit of back-and-forth between the two steps is perfectly natural at this stage. Do what works for you.

When you finish, you should have a list that looks like this:

1.) Goal:
    Significance:
    Measures:
    Action: (*schedule goes here*)
2.) Goal:
    Significance:
    Measures:
    Action: (*schedule goes here*)

3.) Goal:
    Significance:
    Measures:
    Action: (*schedule goes here*)

And so on.

Once you have this, turn to the next section and we'll plan for overcoming obstacles.

Section Four: Anticipating Issues
One step.

In the corporate world, we periodically go through a process called "risk analysis" or "contingency planning." Essentially, this exercise involves asking ourselves what things could go wrong, how to avoid those things if possible, and what we can do if they happen anyway. For some reason I've never understood, almost no one does contingency planning in conjunction with goal-setting. Yet, in the process of working to obtain our goals, it's almost inevitable that something will go sideways. When it does, it frequently throws us completely off-course because we weren't prepared to handle it. So why not acknowledge that we might run into some issues and plan ahead so we'll know what to do when they crop up?

That's what this section (which only contains one step) is about: thinking about what could throw us off-course and developing a plan for dealing with those things.

If you're like most people, you're feeling instinctively anxious right now. That's okay. We're conditioned to fear the idea of problems. But really, running into issues simply means you're moving forward and doing challenging things. A problem is just something to be solved.

That's it. Stressful? Yes, sometimes. But if you work out a possible solution in advance, much less so in the moment.

Before we go over the specifics of this step, we need to talk about a common misapprehension, specifically that anticipating problems is negative thinking and will create self-fulfilling prophecies of doom. Note that this concern is sometimes expressed as embracing positive psychology, however, that's not what positive psychology is about. At all. It's also misinterpreted as "focusing on the positive." In general, focusing on the positive is a good thing, but it can be taken too far. I once worked with a person who spent literal days laboring over a corporate risk analysis in an attempt to "keep it positive." The results were barely intelligible, much less useful. And when, inevitably, some of those risks arose in the course of normal business, this person was completely unprepared to manage them. The way that particular person saw it, however, was simply being positive. This may seem like an extreme example, but I see versions of it all the time.

Here's the most important thing to understand about contingency planning: if you think about what could go wrong now and plan for it, you don't have to worry about it again unless it happens, at which point you'll already have a plan for dealing with it. That means you can focus all your energies on making positive changes in your life and career rather than wasting energy on worry that doesn't help move you forward. This is a much more positive and useful approach. Hence, our next step: Hurdles.

Step Six: H
Hurdles
Core question: What might get in my way and how can I handle it?

Work: Identify potential obstacles and develop a plan for managing them
Why: So you can focus on progress, knowing you have a way to deal with hiccups
Mindset: Realistic, but solutions-focused
End Product: Hurdles and plans for dealing with them, associated with each goal

We've already talked about why this step is important, so let's get to the details about how to do it.

Let's start by addressing terminology, because words really do matter. You'll note that I've used a variety of words to reference potential difficulties: everything from "hiccups" to "issues" to "obstacles." Personally, I'd prefer to use "problem" because I really do see problems as something simply to be solved. I also personally detest the word "challenges" used as a euphemism for problems because it's so overused that everyone knows exactly what it means by now anyway. That said, I concede that we've been acculturated to view problems as horrible, horrible things for which fault must be ascribed and which should be avoided at all costs. So, I do try to avoid using it. If the word "problem" immediately makes you queasy or tense, absolutely don't use it. It's not worth the stress of trying to overcome decades of conditioning unless you are absolutely compelled to take back ownership of the word.

Hence, "Hurdles." This word choice is very intentional, first because it neutralizes the negative cognitive association with words like "problems" and second because you need to focus on things you can actually see coming – and plan to either go around or over. If you let yourself, you can easily get bogged down in (and subsequently demotivated by) trying to imagine all the most horrible things that could go wrong – and by the fact that you have very little control over those things happening. We have dozens of terms for these kinds of things in the corporate world, but I'm going to use "catastrophes" for our discussion. These are the huge things in life that you simply can't do all that much about. If you or a family member experiences a life-threatening injury or illness, your plan is probably going to get revised or put on hold. If the entire economy slides into a major depression, the same thing will happen. That's just life and there's very little we can do about it. For this process, let those things go.

That said, do remember that, while you may be unable to control events, you can control how you react to some of them. You can't control a sudden company downsize, for example, but you can be prepared for such an occurrence by having an updated resume, a plan for coping with the stress, etc. If you strongly suspect this might happen, you'll definitely want to put a lay-off on your list of hurdles.

So, in this step, you're going to do three things:

- Think through each goal and its associated actions
- Write down any hurdles you're likely to encounter
- Write down what you'll do to manage each hurdle

Let's pause and talk about that last one for a moment. There are two ways to deal with hurdles: proactive and reactive. Essentially, you're either attempting to prevent the hurdles from popping up in the first place or figuring out how you'll get over or around them if they do. In most cases, I'm a big fan of proactive moves but, in this case, it sometimes isn't worth it. I see a whole lot of people invest tons of time and energy in trying to prevent from happening something that's a.) virtually inevitable anyway or b.) almost completely out of their control.

Think about the company lay-off, for example. I've seen people go to extreme lengths to try to make themselves too valuable or well-liked to be laid-off when their time would have been much better spent preparing for the inevitable. Similarly, I've seen people invest extraordinary energy trying to save a relationship – be it romantic, platonic, familial, or otherwise – that would be best let go. Does this mean you should always give up on prevention and go straight to coping? Not necessarily. It's a judgement call, one you may need help from a friend, mentor, or therapist to make.

On the flip side, I've seen people sink their valuable time and energy into trying to prevent hurdles that either aren't very likely to crop up or aren't that big a deal to overcome anyway. Sometimes both. If clearing a hurdle won't be all that disruptive, sometimes it's better to just let it come and jump it then. Again, this is a judgement call, one you'll ultimately need to make for yourself.

Here's a little tool that can help you. True risk analysis involves often complicated probability/severity weighting: identifying which things have most impact and which are most probable. The more probable and impactful a potential issue, the more resources you devote to preventing it.

There are all kinds of statistical models and whatnot that you can run to figure this out, but most people setting personal and career goals really only need the graph on the next page.

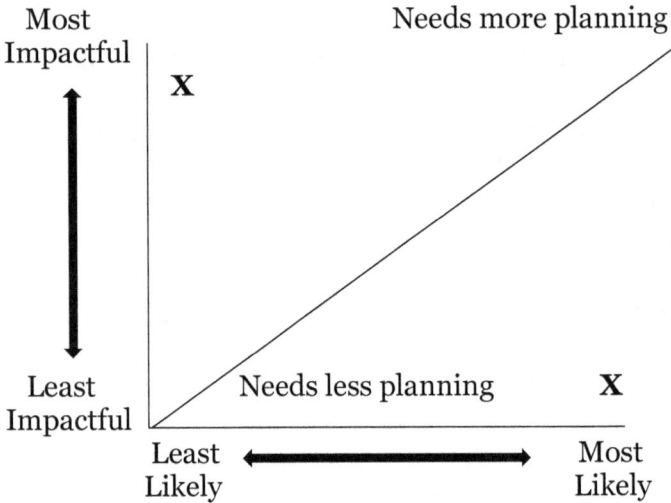

See how that works? The less likely and less impactful the potential hurdle, the less time you need to spend on it (and the more likely that you can plan to deal with it in the moment). The more likely and more impactful the potential hurdle, the more you need to think about it. Those hurdles might require a plan that combines prevention and coping steps. Hurdles that fall in the middle of both factors could go either way. Again, this is a matter of judgement, but looking at potential hurdles this way helps reduce stress for a lot of people.

Do note the two Xes on the graph above because they mark hurdles you need to pay attention to. If a hurdle is very likely to arise, you want to have a plan for it, even if the impact is low. Similarly, if the impact is very high, but it's unlikely to happen, you need to at least be aware of it, simply because it might cause major problems otherwise.

Of course, you do need to keep in mind that, if three minor issues happen all at once, you may suddenly find yourself with a more major issue. If you know this is likely to happen, go ahead and think through it. Otherwise, however, you may simply have to cope with it as it comes. As I said earlier, we can't anticipate everything and this step is not intended to do so. It's merely a way to think through the most likely and help you plan for working through them.

Let's look at a couple of examples.

Remember this one?

Goal 1:	Establish financial security
Significance:	I'll have more control over my life
	I'll be less worried about losing my job
	I'll be able to buy things I want and save for my future
Measures:	Be able to save 20% of my income each month
	Carry zero balances on my credit cards
	Feel less worry about money

Actions: Pay off my debt

Save money

Reduce my monthly bills

Increase my income, either by earning a promotion or finding side work

Sell valuable things I don't use anymore

What might get in this person's way? The most obvious example is an unplanned expense like a major car repair or medical bill that hits before savings are established. So this person might handle hurdles like this:

Goal 1:   Establish financial security

Significance: I'll have more control over my life

I'll be less worried about losing my job

I'll be able to buy things I want and save for my future

Measures: Be able to save 20% of my income each month

Carry zero balances on my credit cards

Feel less worry about money

Actions: Pay off my debt

Save money

Reduce my monthly bills

Increase my income, either by earning a promotion or finding side work

Sell valuable things I don't use anymore

Hurdles: Unplanned major expense - prioritize saving before debt payoff and keep a credit card just for emergencies

How about this one:

Goal 1:	Be healthy
Significance:	I want to live longer
	I want to be able to do more things
	I'll like the way I look and feel
Measures:	20 pounds down
	Cholesterol down 20 points
	Able to run a 15-minute mile More energy
	Able to play with my kids/grandkids/dogs without getting winded
	More rested in the morning
	Fewer sick days/ colds

	Feeling good in my clothes
Actions:	Eat 6 servings of fruits and vegetables per day
	Reduce calories to X per day
	Sleep at least 7 hours per day
	Exercise for X minutes at least X days per week
	Spend X minutes of the day reading/watching TV/playing with my dog/meditating

Hurdles for this person might include a planned cruise or vacation or a muscle strain or other injury that puts their preferred exercise off-limits for a while.

This person might write:

Goal 1:	Be healthy
Significance:	I want to live longer
	I want to be able to do more things
	I'll like the way I look and feel
Measures:	20 pounds down
	Cholesterol down 20 points
	Able to run a 15-minute mile More energy
	Able to play with my

kids/grandkids/dogs without getting winded

More rested in the morning

Fewer sick days/ colds

Feeling good in my clothes

Actions: Eat 6 servings of fruits and vegetables per day

Reduce calories to X per day

Sleep at least 7 hours per day

Exercise for X minutes at least X days per week

Spend X minutes of the day reading/watching TV/playing with my dog/meditating

Hurdles: Winter cruise (yay!) - add a daily thirty-minute walk around the deck to help offset additional calories and return to good habits the day after I return

Potential injury - make sure I stretch even when I don't want to spend the time and make a list of alternate exercises in case I need them

The potential injury is a good way to illustrate the idea of looking at probability and impact. All kinds of factors can affect your probability of injury: your current physical condition, what type of exercise you take on, and any previous injuries, to name a few. Someone with a history of knee problems, for example, will probably want to plan for this hurdle more carefully than someone else might.

Sometimes, clients come back to me at this step and report that they couldn't identify any Hurdles for a particular goal. In some cases, they've simply not thought it through or are having a tough time facing reality. In others, however, there really aren't any major Hurdles to consider. This is always interesting, because it means the most likely thing to get in your way is you, yourself. That's valuable information to have!

One last note: if you think through this deeply enough, you'll quickly realize that losing motivation/energy is a potential hurdle for every goal you'll ever set. Because this is so, I've built in a step specifically to address it, which we'll get to in the next section. For now, you can ignore that hurdle.

Work Time: Hurdles
Task: Identify Hurdles and solutions
Do: Be realistic, but positive
Don't: Let this step steal your motivation. Yes, things may (and probably will) go sideways, but you can handle it and this is a chance to think about how to do so when you aren't in the stress of the moment.

Go ahead and start work. When you finish, your list should look like this:

1.) Goal:
   Significance:
   Measures:
   Action: (*schedule goes here*)
   Hurdles: (*hurdle here*) - (*plan here*)

2.) Goal:
   Significance:
   Measures:
   Action: (*schedule goes here*)
   Hurdles: (*hurdle here*) - (*plan here*)

3.) Goal:
   Significance:
   Measures:
   Action: (*schedule goes here*)
   Hurdles: (*hurdle here*) - (*plan here*)

And so on.

Once you have this, turn to the next section and we'll move into planning for needs.

Section Five: Covering Needs
Two steps.

Did you know failure to plan properly is one of the top reasons new small businesses fail? Another is inadequate funding. People never think they'll need as much as they do, or they tell themselves they'll "make do" with what they have. This isn't a great idea, whether you're starting a business or setting goals. The fact is that, sometimes we need a little help to reach our goals, particularly the big ones. This help can come in many forms:

- Friends, mentors, or other support people
- Classes or other learning opportunities
- Tangibles such as money or other necessary items
- Time in our daily or weekly schedules to devote to pursuing goals

This section, and the two steps involved, are all about figuring out what we need in order to reach the goals we've set – and how to get those things. In Step Seven: Energy, we're going to focus on maintaining and regaining motivation and morale. In Step Eight: Resources, we're going to think through what else you'll need to acquire from somewhere or something outside of yourself. The idea here is to make sure you have the support, knowledge, and other "stuff" you need to reach success. The message is "don't underfund your goals." Finding what we need isn't always easy, but it will be worthwhile. So let's go ahead and start working.

Step Seven: E
Energy
Core question: How will I keep myself going?

Work: Plan to keep your energy and engagement sustained over time
Why: Because we're all still human
Mindset: Realistic but solutions-focused
End Product: Ways to maintain energy throughout the process and regain it if it's lost.

In my 20-plus years of corporate life, I rarely saw companies consider maintaining morale when setting goals or creating a strategic plan. Once I started working with individuals, I discovered the same issue. People simply do not tend to account for the fact that, as human beings, we will inevitably become discouraged, demotivated, or otherwise lose our mental and physical energy. And yet, if we're realistic, we know it will happen. Why not simply accept that fact and plan for it?

For this step, we're going to talk about two kinds of energy sources: maintenance and rescue. Your maintenance energy sources are things you can do every day, week, or month to keep your energy up. Your rescue energy-boosters are those you can deploy if you find yourself suddenly low on motivation or morale. Being asthmatic, I like to compare this to managing that condition. Controller medicines are taken on a regular schedule to help prevent attacks, but most of us also carry a rescue inhaler to deal with sudden issues. Maintenance and rescue energy sources are essentially the same thing.

Your energy-boosters, whether maintenance or rescue, may be very simple things like taking a walk or calling a friend, or they may be more involved, such as taking a trip to a museum or special restaurant – or even heading out of town a few weekends a year. You may also have some overlap between the things you do to maintain and the things you reach for when you've gotten low. That's completely okay.

Identifying your energy sources is a highly personal exercise that requires you to think carefully about what renews you. So, while this step, itself, is fairly simple, the thinking behind it can be intense and somewhat emotional. Again, you want to find things that work for you personally, but below are some starter ideas. This is a highly Googleable topic, so feel free to scan the internet for ideas, too. Also feel free to be very specific. For example, rather than simply writing "call a friend," you might write "call Joe." Instead of writing "get a change of scenery," you might write "work at the coffee shop one afternoon a week."

Thought-Starters:

- Take a walk/hike/bike ride
- Meditate
- List all the things you've accomplished in the last two weeks
- Make a gratitude list

- Read a fun book
- Take your vacation days (and your sick days, when you need them!)
- Read a professional book or article
- Learn about something new
- Call or text with a friend
- Schedule regular time off
- Lunch with a mentor or grab coffee with a colleague
- Take a nap
- Veg in front of the TV for an hour or watch a movie
- Listen to music
- Go somewhere you love to be
- Try a few deep breathing exercises
- Sing with the radio
- Take a play break (or date) with your kids or pets

Tip for introverts: choose some things that involve other people and some things that give you alone time. Most of my introvert clients tend to choose only the latter initially. While this isn't surprising as introverts tend to restock energy best alone, it can be problematic. Sometimes, we really do need someone we trust to pull us out of a funk or readjust unproductive thinking. Make sure to ask yourself who that someone could be for you.

Work Time: Energy

Task: Identify ways to renew your energy

Do: Include things to do for yourself, people you can call, etc.

Don't: Assume this step is unnecessary and skip it!

You want to identify a total of three to five things you can do on a regular basis to maintain your personal energy and another three to five that you can do to regain energy if you hit a low point. (Note: more than five is fine for this one.) Most people put their energy sources in one general list at the end of their goal plans, but occasionally I meet someone who wants to choose energy-boosters for each individual goal. Either way is fine, depending on what works best for you, and I've provided a sample of what each might look like below. When you finish, your list should look like one of the following:

End-of-Plan Option

1.) Goal:
   Significance:
   Measures:
   Action: (*schedule goes here*)
   Hurdles: (*hurdle here*) - (*plan here*)

2.) Goal:
   Significance:
   Measures:
   Action: (*schedule goes here*)
   Hurdles: (*hurdle here*) - (*plan here*)

3.) Goal:
   Significance:
   Measures:
   Action: (*schedule goes here*)
   Hurdles: (*hurdle here*) - (*plan here*)

Energy Sources:
1
2
3
4
5

Goal-by-Goal Option

1.) Goal:
   Significance:
   Measures:
   Action: (*schedule goes here*)
   Hurdles: (*hurdle here*) - (*plan here*)
   Energy Sources:

2.) Goal:
   Significance:
   Measures:
   Action: (*schedule goes here*)
   Hurdles: (*hurdle here*) - (*plan here*)
   Energy Sources:

3.) Goal:
   Significance:
   Measures:
   Action: (*schedule goes here*)
   Hurdles: (*hurdle here*) - (*plan here*)
   Energy Sources:

When you finish, turn to the next step.

Step Eight: R
Resources
Core question: What do I need to complete my actions/meet my goals?

Work: Identify what you need and where you can find it
Why: So you're equipped to do your best
Mindset: Realistic and solutions-focused
End Product: Needs and resources for each goal

In addition to making sure you have enough energy to go for your goals, it's important to think about what other things you'll need. Resources you need may be tangible or intangible. This is a two-part process. The first is figuring out what you need. This concept is pretty straightforward, so let's go straight to a few examples.

Remember the "be healthy" goal? A person with this goal might need a gym membership or in-home equipment, recipe ideas, a calorie-counting or exercise-tracking app, a meditation or other class, books, etc. But they might also need things like a consultation with a nutritionist, a personal trainer, or another professional. In addition, they're going to need things like dedicated time for mental and physical wellness, possibly care for a child or other dependent, and maybe an accountability system.

What about our goal-setter who wanted to establish job security? This person might need additional training, a subscription to a professional journal, advice from a mentor, etc. but also time to read the journals and funding for the training. Similarly, the person looking to establish financial security might need an appointment with a financial advisor, a budget, and a way to track spending, but also a list of free or low-cost entertainment and a way to establish new sources of income.

Again, this is a fairly simple idea, but you will need to think critically about your goals and actions, which can be challenging. Do note that visualization works well here for many people. Picture, in your head, what it would look like to execute your actions. What are you using or carrying with you? Who has given you advice? What knowledge do you have in the vision that you don't currently have in reality? Don't forget to consider any mental and emotional resources you may need, such as a support network, a way to manage stress or imposter syndrome, etc.

Once you know what you need, you'll turn to figuring out how and where to get it. This is often the tougher part for many people, but it is doable (and important). Let's go back to health. This person needs an accountability system, but there are lots of ways to do that. For some, it's a simple matter of keeping a personal record or journal. Others prefer having a program or app that tracks data. Still others need to be accountable to someone outside themselves, which could be friends and family or a professional like a trainer or coach. The key is to figure out which you think will work for you, then identify where you can find it. Can you ask a friend to be your accountability partner or would you rather check the app store? How will you get the accountability system you need so you can successfully pursue your goals?

Some questions to ask yourself if you get stuck:

- Who do I know that might have experience in this area?
- What internet searches can I do to find information?
- Who can help me make time to do what I need to do?
- Where can I find any funds that I need?

Work Time: Resources

Task: List the resources you need to achieve your goals/execute your actions, and decide how you will get them
Do: Be specific when possible
Don't: Let yourself get overwhelmed.

Let's go ahead and take a careful look at your plan and think through what you need and where/how you can get it. Note that, in the process of completing this step, you may find you need to add actions that address actually obtaining what you need. For example, if you realize you need a reliable source of advice about a specific topic (health, nutrition, your industry, finances, etc.), and you don't have one now, add "Identify and secure a reliable source of advice" to your actions list. If you need new hand weights and a yoga mat, create an action of acquiring them. If you need a new resume, add an action item for either revamping yours or hiring a professional to do so. Whatever you need, make sure you actually take steps to get it. If you find you need far more than you can realistically get right now, you might need to back up and make getting those things your first priority. This may mean adjusting your schedule for other actions and placing the actions that will secure your needed resources first.

When you finish, your list should look like this:

1.) Goal:
    Significance:
    Measures:
    Action: (*schedule goes here*)
    Hurdles: (*hurdle here*) - (*plan here*)
    Energy Sources:
    Resources: (*what I need*) - (*where I can get it*)

2.) Goal:
    Significance:
    Measures:
    Action: (*schedule goes here*)

Hurdles: (*hurdle here*) - (*plan here*)
Energy Sources:
Resources: (*what I need*) - (*where I can get it*)

3.) Goal:
Significance:
Measures:
Action: (*schedule goes here*)
Hurdles: (*hurdle here*) - (*plan here*)
Resources:

Energy Sources:

Once you've completed Resources, we'll move to the final step and complete your plan, then talk a bit about how to implement it.

Section Six: Rewards
One step.

We've finally arrived at the last step in our goal-setting process, and it's an important one for two reasons. The first is the more obvious one: it's important to reward yourself for hard work. This is true no matter what kind of environment you're in and what kinds of goals you're setting. It's all well and good to say that a job well done is its own reward, but let's be realistic. It's better to have an actual reward (or more than one). It just is. The rewards you identify will help keep you motivated when the actions get tough or your schedule gets behind. You're simply giving yourself another reason to stay engaged with your goals as the weeks and months go on.

The second reason is that thinking about rewards ties us back to the big vision we worked on in the first three steps. So many times, people bog down in the details, get caught up in concrete actions and "checking things off the list," that they forget why they're doing it. But if there isn't something pretty exciting waiting for you, why even bother trying to reach that goal? Isn't that the point of goals? To go after something you want, something that makes your life better and helps you be who and what you want to be? That's exciting, right? It should be.

That's why this last step is represented by an exclamation mark. What we're going to do now is figure out the exciting things waiting for you. Let's begin.

Step Nine: Rewards!
This is the ! at the end
Core question: What will I get for reaching my goals?

Work: Identify rewards and benefits
Why: Motivation and reconnection with the big picture
Mindset: Optimistic and engaged
End Product: List of rewards associated with reaching each goal

We've already talked about why we need rewards, so let's spend a minute on what a reward is. Like goals, this is a less obvious answer than it might at first appear. Strictly speaking, a reward is anything you get for accomplishing a task, reaching a milestone, etc. What's important to understand is that there are two types of rewards: those that come to you as a natural consequence of the achievement and those you actively give yourself (or others) for reaching the goal.

Most clients tend to think automatically of one of these – and completely ignore the other. One camp focuses on the improvements in their life, the increase in their bank account, etc. that will automatically happen once the goal is achieved. The other camp focuses on created rewards such as trips, days off, a special purchase, etc. Neither of these are wrong but, in my experience, you get the best results when you identify some of each. So that's your task in this step. Remember that your rewards can be tangible or intangible, though I always recommend including at least one tangible for each goal. Tip: try visualizing what success looks like if you're having a hard time with the intangibles.

I do want to mention one specific benefit that shows up on a lot of lists: confidence. Most people who pick up this book will have been down the goal-setting road before, and they may not have found great success. That can wear on your confidence over time, make you feel like setting goals is pointless because you never reach them anyway. The reverse is also true. The more times you achieve your goals – and the more times you reward yourself and truly celebrate the success – the more your confidence will grow. So please don't skip this step, either now or when the time comes to enjoy your reward. And if you're low on confidence in this area right now, I strongly urge you to set mini-rewards for at least some of your actions to help build it back up – and to keep you moving along and engaged!

One other important note. Be very careful of absolutism here. What I mean by this is, don't get so focused on meeting every single measure by the exact date you set in order to "prove" your success and "deserve" your reward that you never actually get the good stuff. And don't let goal changes keep you from ever celebrating achievements. Remember, things outside your control can easily happen – and sometimes life just doesn't go as planned. Make sure you're planning to reward yourself for the energy and work invested rather than just the outcome.

Work Time: Rewards!

Task: Decide what you'll get when you reach your goals
Do: Include tangible and intangible rewards
Don't: Skip this step. It's more important than people realize.

And here we are. Your final goal-setting activity. Your last task is to choose how you'll be rewarded for reaching your goals. Don't forget that you can also plug in mini-rewards for completing actions. This works very well for many people, especially when working with long-term goals or actions. When you finish this step, your plan will be complete and should look something like this:

1.) Goal:
  Significance:
  Rewards:
  Measures:
  Action: (*schedule goes here*)
  Hurdles: (*hurdle here*) - (*plan here*)
  Resources: (*what I need*) - (*where I can get it*)

2.) Goal:
  Significance:
  Rewards:

Measures:
Action: (*schedule goes here*)
Hurdles: (*hurdle here*) - (*plan here*)
Resources: (*what I need*) - (*where I can get it*)

3.) Goal:
Significance:
Rewards:
Measures:
Action: (*schedule goes here*)
Hurdles: (*hurdle here*) - (*plan here*)
Resources: (*what I need*) - (*where I can get it*)

Energy Sources:
1
2
3
4
5

You may notice that I like to put Rewards just under Significance. This keeps it visible when you go back and look at your plan. But if you prefer to put Rewards after Resources, that's okay, too. Do what makes most sense to you. At this point, I recommend you write out a clean copy of your plan, either longhand or in an electronic document. It's time to finalize (for now – remember you can always edit) and then we'll talk about how you can start living with your plan. When you're ready, turn to the final section of the book and we'll talk about what comes next.

Section Seven: Now What?

At this stage, people inevitably (and reasonably) ask, "now what?" It's a good question. You've got this beautiful new plan, you hopefully have a clear picture of what you want and ways to work toward it, and you're excited. But what do you do tomorrow?

Here's my suggestion for the immediate future, particularly if you wrote your plan during a compressed time period: walk away and ignore it for a week, maybe two. Then come back and read it again, both to make sure it still makes sense and to re-engage with your vision for your future. Planning goals can be draining, physically and mentally, and it won't hurt anything for you to take a little time away.

Do come back, though. You've worked too hard to let it all go to waste. And, frankly, I see people walk away from great plans and never look back all the time. Organizations and companies, large and small, are notorious for putting incredible work into a plan, then sticking it in a drawer and ignoring it until the next planning period. Don't do that. Your plan should be a living document, something you engage with on a regular basis. Otherwise, there's absolutely no point in making one to begin with.

So, how do you, in concrete terms, turn the plan from a static document to a living one? Two ways: Working the plan on a daily/weekly basis and Scheduled assessment

Working the Plan

To some degree, how you incorporate your goals and actions day-to-day will depend on how you prefer to manage your schedule and how far in advance you can/prefer to set it. I personally use the following system:

- A one-year plan document
- A three-month list of projects to focus on, posted on my office wall
- A one-month short-list of priorities on my desk, and
- A paper planner in which I schedule and keep track of my daily and weekly tasks, meetings, and priorities

Every three months, I assess my annual plan, make any necessary adjustments, and transfer the next quarter's activities/priorities to the wall. At the end of each month, I transfer the next month's priorities to the mini-whiteboard on my desk (it's propped up so I can see it at all times). I then go into my planner, plug in any known meetings/commitments for the next month first, and then begin scheduling in time for that month's tasks/priorities as identified on my monthly list. Every week, either Sunday evening or first thing Monday morning, I spend twenty to thirty minutes comparing the monthly list on my desk to my scheduled activities for the week, just to make sure I've made time for all of my top priorities without overscheduling myself (which includes blocking out a certain amount of time for unexpected things). If not, I adjust my planner accordingly. I also look back at the previous week to make sure I've carried forward any action items I didn't, for one reason or another, get to as planned.

Important: when I carry forward an item the first time, I put the notation "CF1" next to it. The second time, I write "CF2." I never carry forward an item for the third time without thinking through why I'm not getting to it. Sometimes, it's because I don't really need to do it anymore. Sometimes, it just isn't as high a priority as other things on my list at the moment and needs to be pushed out to a less busy time. Sometimes I realize I need a resource before I can complete it. Sometimes, I'm just flat-out avoiding it for some reason. Once I know the reason, I can decide how to handle the task.

The system may sound bulky, but it really doesn't take all that much time to manage, and it gives me an opportunity to reconnect to my overall goals often enough to keep from getting completely bogged down in the daily grind and giving up. It also ensures that my big-picture priorities stay top-of-mind and helps me continue to make forward progress – even when that progress gets interrupted or doesn't go as quickly as I want it to.

I like this system. It took me three years to figure out, but it works really well for me – and it's worked well for most of my clients who have tried something similar. But it's not the only way. You can use virtually any day-to-day planning system that makes sense to you. The critical components of a workable system are these:

- An annual (or longer) plan document
- A built-in way to assess your plan every three months
- A way to identify your top priorities on a monthly basis
- A way to make sure you incorporate relevant action items into each day or week
- A mechanism for identifying tasks you never seem to get to so you can figure out why and what to do about them

As you decide what kind of system you want to create for yourself, be aware of the power of keeping an ongoing record. I used to simply make weekly to-do lists, then throw them away them after I wrote the next week's. The problem was that, after a while, I couldn't remember what I'd done anymore. That's fine if you're focused on just getting stuff done. But if you want to stay connected to the bigger picture, it doesn't work so well. I use a planner now so that, if I get frustrated with "running behind" the often aggressive schedule I've set for myself, I can go back and look at everything I *have* gotten done rather than focusing on what I *haven't*. On the flip side, I can go back and look at periods during which I genuinely don't get much done and figure out why. That makes my future planning much more accurate and effective. That's strategic. I'm not saying you can't use to-do lists instead of a planner. I just recommend that you date each list and file them at the end of the week instead of tossing them out.

One other pro tip: when you find yourself faced with a task you really don't want to do, remind yourself why you're doing it. I don't mean the "I have to because it's on the list" reason, I mean the real reason, the one that prompted you to put it on the list in the first place. You can also remind yourself about the reward(s) completing the task will move you toward. Motivation matters. You've gone to the trouble of identifying motivators for yourself. Use them. And don't forget to schedule your maintenance energy sources – and deploy the rescue ones when you need them.

Assessment

Regardless of which system you use on a daily basis, I recommend everyone set aside an hour or so to assess their plans every three months. Again, remember that this is not an evaluation of your performance. It's an assessment of how well your plan is working and where you are in relation to reaching your goals. Before you ask whether you're doing the work you need to do, ask whether you're following the right plan.

Once a year, give yourself a day or two – or a few hours each day for a week or two – to look in-depth at what you want for the next year (or longer) and make sure you have a plan that reflects those goals. To do this, you'll essentially repeat the process outlined in this book. However, if you went into this round thoughtfully and took your time with it, you'll probably find that your goals and significances – as well as many, if not all of your energy sources – don't change very much. That means most of your focus will be on double-checking your measures, hurdles, resources, and rewards, and adjusting where needed, as well as on setting new actions and schedules.

The first step in assessment is asking whether you've made the progress you planned to make. If so, you're in great shape! Read through your plan to reconnect, and also to add any new measures, actions, hurdles, energy sources, and resources you've identified. At the same time, on a separate page, write down any actions you've finished, what progress you've made toward reaching your measures, what hurdles you overcame in the past three months, and which energy sources you found most useful. This is your assessment report for the quarter. Don't skip this part! This is what I like to call "celebrating progress in process." Give yourself credit for what you've accomplished before you jump straight into tackling the next task. Never take progress for granted. In so doing, you take yourself for granted. Also, note that assessment reports have a functional use as well. When you go into your next annual (or longer) planning period, you'll be able to look back at these notes and see what worked and what didn't. That's incredibly valuable information.

If you aren't where you want to be on one or more goals, ask yourself the following eight questions, in the following order. Remember to think critically about the plan, without being critical of yourself. This is about making sure you have the right roadmap.

1.) Is my goal still the same? (If not, what is it now?)
2.) Are these the right actions? (If not, what should they be?)
3.) Am I taking the actions as scheduled? (If not, why not and what do I need to change?)
4.) Is the schedule I set really reasonable? (If not, what is?)

5.) Am I executing the actions in a quality way? (If not, why not? Do I need to adjust my schedule?)

6.) Am I scheduling my maintenance energy sources and actually doing them? (If not, why not?)

7.) Am I using my rescue energy sources when I need them? (If not, why not?)

8.) Do I have all the resources I need? (If not, what are they and how will I get them?)

If your answer to any of the eight questions is "no," adjust your goal plan accordingly. Then complete the assessment report described above, even if you feel you only have a few positives to report. Again I say: never take progress for granted.

Don't get frustrated if you find yourself adjusting a lot in the first couple of assessment periods. This is extremely common and will get better. Don't give up. The system works, but you'll need some time and practice to get it down. Never forget that this is a very different way of thinking about goals and it's okay to have a learning curve. FYI, I can tell you right now that the number one problem you're likely to face is that you've been too unrealistic in setting actions and schedules. Everyone always wants to do everything *right this second*. People hate facing the fact that almost everything takes more time, effort, and patience than we want it to. Unless you can alter the laws of physics, you need to learn to alter your own expectations. Otherwise, you'll just keep getting frustrated and looking for ways to achieve the unachievable. That's a complete waste of time. Isn't it better to face reality now and start moving forward, even if it's more slowly than you like, rather than keep trying to do the impossible for the next five years and *then* face facts? How much farther will you be in five years if you simply start crawling toward your goals today?

Now, if the answer to all eight above questions is "yes," but you're still not where you want to be, or if you can't figure out why you aren't taking your actions/using your energy sources/etc., you actually do have an execution problem, not a planning problem. At this point, you may need to seek more personalized help in moving forward, whether from friends, a professional coach, a therapist, or personal strategy books and blogs that focus on getting unstuck. Problems in planning almost always boil down to the same small set of issues. Execution problems, on the other hand, can have a myriad of sources and require more individualized attention to work through. If you've gone through the effort of planning well, please go to the effort of finding someone who can help you execute. Your goals are worth it.

Onward!

And there you have it: a detailed, workable, goal plan designed to help you get where you want to go. From here, the ball is in your court. Work the plan, use the plan, and don't forget to assess on schedule. Your goals are yours for the taking. Go forth and smash them!

30-Day Plan (Aggressive Model)

Note: this schedule will require you to spend at least 60-90 minutes working on your plan every day. You may need to allow yourself more days to work this process, based on your schedule. I do NOT recommend spending less time than indicated below on any section/task.

Reminder: complete pre-work in Section One first. Do not begin until you've done so.

Day 1	Read Section Two intro Read Step One: Goals, through "Brainstorm Big Goals" task Brainstorm initial goal list
2 & 3	Revisit goal list and add any new thoughts
4	Read "Wishes" section of Step One: Goals Complete "Weed Out Wishes" task
5	Read "Not-Goals" section of Step One: Goals Complete "No More Not-Goals" task
6	Read Step Two: Significance through "What's Your Why" task
6 & 7	Complete "What's Your Why" task
8	Read Step Two: Significance, "Have-Tos" Complete "Ditching No-Choice Whys" task
9	Read Step Two: Significance, "Shoulds" Complete "Spotting Shoulds" task
10	Read Step Two: Significance, "Clarifying Your Intent" section

10 & 11	Complete "Clarifying Your Intent" task
12	Read Step Two: Significance, "Looking for Patterns" section
12 & 13	Complete "Looking for Patterns" task
14	Read Step Three: Measures through "Identifying Measures" task
14-15	Complete "Identifying Measures" task
16	Read Step Three: Measures "Finalizing Your Goals" section Complete "Finalizing Your Goals" task
17	Read all of Section Three (includes Step Four: Actions and Step Five: Schedule)
17-20	Complete "Adding the Details" task
21	Read all of Section Four: Anticipating Issues (includes Step Six: Hurdles)
21 -23	Complete "Hurdles" task
24	Read Section Five intro and Step Seven: Energy Complete "Energy" task
25	Read Step Eight: Resources
25 -27	Complete "Resources" task
28	Read all of Section Six
28 & 29	Complete "Rewards" task
30	Read Section Seven: Now What?

About the Author

Maggie Worth has three superpowers: writing, learning, and strategy. She makes her living as a speaker, consultant, workshop leader, and freelance writer, but she's also a dog schmuck, Sinatra fan, perpetual student, and nacho connoisseur. A born strategist who sees patterns and connections where most people don't, and can use those insights to create workable, effective solutions to real-world problems, she's spent more than 20 years helping people, businesses, and organizational leaders figure out what they want, why they want it, and how to get there.

Learn more at WheatGermStrategy.com.

The Goal SMASHER! system has been versioned for the following audiences:

Small Business Owners and Entrepreneurs
Corporations and Organizations
Fiction Writers